The Secrets of
SUCCESSFUL
DIRECT
RESPONSE
MARKETING

About the author

Frank Jefkins has applied direct response techniques to his own business for twenty years, selling books, training courses and distance learning courses by mail on a world basis. His mail order book service has sold books to seventy countries, and his Summer School has attracted management participants from forty-two countries since 1980. He has also worked as a copywriter for direct mail houses, and for several years produced direct mail shots to sell advertisement space in magazines. He holds the CAM Diploma with Honours. In 1988, in its centenary year, the London Chamber of Commerce awarded him an Honorary Fellowship. He pioneered the LCC Marketing Diploma, and is the chief examiner. He has lectured widely and has run courses in twenty-four countries. He has over twenty books in print, his major work being his *International Dictionary of Marketing and Communication*.

Books in the series

The Secrets of
SUCCESSFUL DIRECT RESPONSE MARKETING

Frank Jefkins

BScEcon, BA(Hons), MCAM, ABC, FAIE
FIPR, FLCC, FInstSMM, MInstM

Heinemann Professional Publishing

This book is dedicated to my wife Frances

Heinemann Professional Publishing Ltd
Halley Court, Jordan Hill, Oxford OX2 8EJ

OXFORD LONDON MELBOURNE AUCKLAND SINGAPORE
IBADAN NAIROBI GABORONE KINGSTON

First published 1988
First published as a paperback edition 1990

British Library Cataloguing in Publication Data

Jefkins, Frank
The Secrets of successful direct response marketing
1. Direct mail marketing
I. Title
658.872

ISBN 0 434 90903 3

Photoset by Deltatype Ltd, Ellesmere Port, Cheshire
Printed in Great Britain by
Billings of Worcester Ltd

Contents

Preface

Direct response marketing is big business. I have used it myself over the past 20 years to promote four businesses, both nationally and internationally.

Advertising is often criticized, direct mail is frequently maligned, and door-to-door distribution sometimes invokes contempt.

This book is not just a textbook laying down the rules. It criticizes the abuses of direct marketing which make it all the harder for you to succeed. At the same time it invites you to decide how best direct marketing can be applied profitably to your business.

How can you invest in economical and successful direct mail marketing? This book sets out to tell you. You may not always agree with what is said, but it will make you think more critically about what is most likely to work for you.

1   How to avoid junk mail

What is junk mail?

Some people regard it as any unsolicited commercial mail. They probably don't like any kind of advertising, and pretend it never influences them to buy anything. Without advertising, modern industrial society would not exist. Without advertising we would be back to a feudal age of market stalls, small shops, small towns and no factories.

John Rowe of the Spastics Society, in a letter printed in *Direct Response*, wrote: 'Unprofitable mailings are junk, and profitable mailings are not. It really is as simple as that.'

Harassed recipients of junk mail often find it extremely difficult to get themselves off mailing lists. However, one proven way is to write 'deceased' on the envelope and return it to sender.

One of the biggest causes of junk mail has been Margaret Thatcher's thirst for privatization. The vast new share registers for British Gas, British Telecom, TSB and other sell-share offers have provided indiscriminate database mailing lists for scores of financial direct response mailings. Consequently, humble first-time investors – so beloved by the Government – have been avalanched by mailings for sophisticated propositions often beyond the understanding of humble investors. The familiar investment broker has become a 'financial adviser' who may pretend he is not really selling you insurance but is planning your financial future. He's also planning his, of course.

The foot-in-the-door salesman of yesteryear has become the persuasive letterbox marketer. Privatization has probably created more junk mail than anything else. It gives another meaning to 'market forces'.

Similarly, umpteen duplicated mailings were delivered, week by week, by Royal Life during their sledge-hammer launch of unit trusts just before the Stock Exchange crash of 1987. No wonder Jeff Partridge in his *Guardian* 'Weekend money' feature wrote: 'Royal Life has spent almost £6 million trying to seduce us. But think before you succumb.' The headline was 'Royal flush'. Press and TV advertising was also used.

With some 1500 million direct mail items being mailed a year at a cost of about £500 million, and an annual increase of 20 per cent, it is not surprising that there is a lot of junk mail about. In recent years the banks have tripled their use of the medium, setting up special direct marketing departments like that of Nat-West. Since the Big Bang in October 1986, financial houses – particularly insurance companies with their bonds and unit trusts – have concentrated on direct response marketing through the press, television and direct mail. Much of it has been aimed at small investors, seeking to induce them to convert their building society savings into something more 'profitable'. And even after October 1987 they were selling deflated shares in strong economies.

It is a formidable torrent of advertising. Well, advertising is said to reflect the economic prosperity of a country, so perhaps the spate of direct mail offers indicates an optimistic upturn. It also shows a more economic use of advertising, that is of advertising which is less costly and better targeted.

The British are always critical of advertising, especially when it is thrust under their noses as direct mail shots and doorstoppers certainly are. You don't have to read press advertisements or posters, you can go to the loo when the telly commercials are on, but the direct mail shot is on the mat or on the desk. *Can its very power and presence be its own undoing?*

Some of the insurance companies have not been very clever when offering their supposedly 'limited' special offers, mailing the same person repeatedly. I mentioned this in the following letter (published in *Direct Response* in July 1987) about one of the causes of repetitive junk mail: careless keying of computer keyboards.

Keyboard carelessness

Dear Sir

Direct mail often earns the name of junk mail simply because its mailing list creators are careless.

Every morning I receive direct mail shots and they contribute the bulk of my dustbin contents. Yet I have run a successful business for 20 years which has been dependent on direct mail.

One of the secrets of my success is that I never use an outside service.

During the past four weeks I have received some 20 offers of the Sun Life 'limited' bond! They must have wasted a fortune on mis-mailings. Shoals of Mr Tebbit's begging letters have arrived. This week two firms have written to me as Mr Jeffs, and Kompass have sent me two shots, one addressed to Jepkins and the other to Jepherson. An insurance broker has mailed me in triplicate.

The reason for all these multiple mailings is that I have been addressed as Jenkins, Jeffrey, Jeffreys, Jeffery, Jeffries, Jephkins, Jepkins, Jifkins and numerous other variations which must defy de-duplication.

Yet, presumably, my personal name or business name has been taken from share registers, membership lists, directories and other sources where it appears correctly. Slovenly keying is the culprit. List compilers and list brokers are the creators of junk mail.

To these culprits must be added those blanket mailers to whom it never occurs that someone who has been a member or customer for years finds it irritating to be repeatedly mailed as a prospect. Among the worst antagonizers are American Express, who seem to be ignorant of the identity of their cardholders.

Frank Jefkins

What is one to make of the following piece of addressing from our most inept mailers, American Express?

American Express Europe Limited
Card Services
P.O. Box 68
Amex House, Edward Street
Brighton, England BN2 1YL

Ms. Janet Pigott
Frank Jenkins School of Pub Re
84 Ballerds Way
Croydon
CR2 7LA

What attracts the better type of customer?
The better type of Card.

Dear Ms. Pigott,

If I asked you to describe your ideal customer, who would it be?
Someone with more money to spend than the average person? Who
spends more than most customers on hardback and paperback books?
And someone with no pre-set limit on how much they spend in your
bookstore?

I have a simple suggestion that could attract one million
customers like this into your store. Accept this invitation to
welcome American Express Cardmembers into your store and enjoy
increased sales.

American Express Cardmembers earn more

By accepting the American Express Card you'll be
welcoming one million Cardmembers who earn twice as much

*National
average income
£10,740*

as most people in the UK. Average UK
earnings are £10,740 ... Amex
Cardmembers earn on average
£25,000.

Cardmember average income £25,000

And they spend more too

You should make an average sale of £30 worth of books
to American Express Cardmembers. That's much more
than other customers spend.

What's more, American Express Cardmembers are keen
booklovers - and they closely match the typical book
buyer profile. In fact they could be just the type
of customer you'd like to see browsing in your store.

As you know, books are usually impulse buys - which is
another reason why it pays to accept the American
Express Card. Because 35% of Cardmembers'
purchases are bought on impulse. And
when it comes to choosing
the latest best-selling
paperbacks, glossy reference

Average Card transaction on books £30

books and hardbacks as gifts for family and
friends, the American Express Card has no
pre-set spending limit. This gives Cardmembers
extra financial freedom to choose just what they want.

35% of all retail purchases are impulse buys

The sign that says 'Hello' to over 1,000,000 UK customers

In the UK alone over 1,000,000 people carry, and choose to pay with
the American Express Card.

In fact research has shown that Cardmembers prefer to shop where
they see the American Express 'Cards Welcome' sign.

American Express Europe Limited is incorporated with limited liability in the State of Delaware U.S.A.

The majority of our Cardmembers are aged between 25 and 45 - so you'll see why this represents a large market of young, free spending customers for you to profit from.

Say hello to thousands of wealthy overseas visitors too

Cards Welcome

American Express have 27 million Cardmembers Worldwide, and many of them frequently travel overseas - so accepting the American Express Card

Over one million people carry the Card in the UK.

could represent an important source of potential new customers for you.

We encourage spending through national advertising

Throughout the world American Express spend heavily on encouraging our Cardmembers to use the Card whenever they make a purchase.

This includes active support programmes for outlets like yours to help bring more profits your way. So when you welcome the American Express Card, you'll benefit from high spending Cardmembers who are constantly reminded of the benefits of using the Card.

A high percentage of foreign spending is charged to the American Express Card.

Accept our invitation to welcome the Card

When you choose to accept the Card, our Cardmembers will be looking out for the familiar white and blue sign. We'll supply you with these in addition to imprinters, decals and all the stationery your size of business requires.

And if you haven't considered welcoming the American Express Card into your

78% of all Cardmembers look for the 'Cards Welcome' sign

store before, you may have some questions you'd like to ask. That's why I'd like to invite you to accept our free consultation. Simply complete and return the enclosed reply card. Your local area manager will arrange a convenient time to see you.

Accept a better card and open your store to <u>over 1 million</u> 'better types' of customer by returning the reply card today.

Yours sincerely

John Petersen

John Petersen

PS Remember, every day, high spending customers could be passing your store by because you don't accept the American Express Card - don't waste anymore time - reply today.

Ms Janet Pigott
Frank Jenkins School of Pub Re
84 Ballerds Way
Croydon
CR2 7LA

There is no such person as Ms Janet Pigott. The name is Jefkins, not Jenkins, and what is 'Pub Re'? The street is spelt 'Ballards' not 'Ballerds'. The town is South Croydon, which meant that the Post Office had to write 'South' on the envelope and transfer the letter to another sorting office.

Perhaps all that was intended to arouse curiosity and get the letter opened, which of course it did. The personalized letter was addressed to the non-existent Ms Pigott and addressed her as if she was running a bookshop and should welcome American Express Cardmembers. The School does not have a bookshop but runs courses, and the four-page pictorial letter about booklovers and 'your store' was irrelevant. How does a large organization and a great user of direct response get so many things wrong?

Maybe 500 million instead of 1500 million mail shots can do the job as effectively and less expensively. It may be a more successful and cheaper medium if there is a lot less of it!

Make no mistake, direct response marketing *does* work wonders. It depends on how you do it. The great mail order houses of the USA and Canada have been doing it for more than a century. I have run a successful international business for 20 years, using direct mail. I could not have done it with press advertising. Three reasons for its success have been a one-piece mailer; limited and selective mailing lists compiled in-house; and careful timing. None of these elementary techniques is applied by the junk mailers, including some of those already criticized for their proliferation of shots and shot contents.

Public relations suffers from its own form of junk mail, resulting in what is known as the 'adversarial situation' between the media and PROs. Editors are inundated not only by badly written news releases, but by ones which have been wrongly timed or misdirected by lazy and unskilled compilation of mailing lists.

The principles of direct mail apply to news releases, but a lot of PR people are ignorant of them. As a result, they indulge in the blanket mailing of rubbish. If out of a hundred news releases only one is published, that is a hit rate of 1 per cent; whereas if one release is sent to the only journal likely to publish it, and that journal does, that is a hit rate of 100 per cent. The junk mail consists of the irrelevant ninety-nine releases.

That is why the careful selection or culling of lists is so vital in direct response marketing. The problem is that sometimes one cannot always know which names to eliminate. Even some of those who complain about junk mail may in fact prove to be customers in the long run.

Since there is no doubt about the success of direct mail, in both its effectiveness and its economy, we must consider the variety of techniques which abound. Junk mail results from the wrong use of techniques, and while it is impossible to placate the determined critic, many of the complaints and condemnations are avoidable. At least, *you* can try to avoid them.

So, which methods are most likely to work for you? Which are the least likely to evoke the contemptuous dismissal of your shots as junk mail? You will probably find that if the wrong technique is used it will be resented, but if it is the right one it will be welcomed and responded to. The irony of direct response marketing is that some of it is too clever by half – but which half? Send a man a superb holiday brochure when he has just received a Christmas bonus and he will love you, but mail it when he has already spent his bonus and he will hate you. And you could have got the timing right but a Post Office strike ruined it.

Again, it may be a good idea to provoke action through something like a fruit machine scratch card which appeals to curiosity and greed. But if some mystery offer is sealed and perforated edges have to be ripped off, the recipient may find this tiresome and retort 'to hell with this!' Reactions have to be anticipated, and better still tested. There are gimmicks galore in direct marketing, as we shall see later in this book. Some of them are bloody marvellous, and some are a bloody nuisance.

So, direct marketing is full of opportunities if you use your brains. You don't just stuff things in envelopes and stuff the lot in a Post Office letterbox.

There is a very big public relations element in direct mail, for it can make or mar the perceived image of your organization. An image cannot be created, only deserved. Junk mail can destroy it.

It comes down to simple planning and to the definition of policy about your style of mailing. You need to be consistent, and consistency can exploit that secret of all successful advertising – *repetition*. Your style – the design of your envelopes, letterheading, order form, leaflet, catalogue – should characterize your firm. Stick to it and people will stick to you. This style can be your *corporate identity*, like that of a store, petrol pump, motor-car manufacturer, brewer or airline which are all instantly recognizable by their logo, colour, typography or livery.

There are five basic rules to planning a direct marketing campaign:

Identify your market Precisely to whom are you aiming to sell? This can vary from one product or service to another.

Determine the kind of response you are seeking   An order with cash? An order against invoice? An enquiry? A telephone call? A visit to a supplier?

Have a good reason for provoking response   Is it the originality or topicality of the offer, the value for money price, or the quality of the product? There must be a good and clear reason why they should respond. No why, no buy!

Determine the location of your market   Is it local, regional, national or international? What effect does this have on, say, prices, payments, guarantees, refunds, goods despatch times, packing, documentation and methods of carriage?

Determine timing   There are often times to avoid, such as Saturdays, bank holidays and festivals; maybe half-day closings or school holidays; and with overseas mailings, periods like Ramadan in Muslim countries. With foreign mailings you will have to consider how long it will take mail to reach its destination. Some places can be reached in days, others in weeks, and it may depend on whether you rely on the Post Office or use a commercial service.

Again, the postage rate, and whether or not you use a rebate service, will affect postal delivery. Similarly some door-to-door distributions can be completed in three days, others in two weeks, according to the distributor you hire. For off-the-page promotions or inserts you will have to book issues for future dates, maybe weeks ahead, but your ability to service orders will have to match insertion dates.

Timing has therefore to combine your production of promotional material, how long it will take prospects to receive your message, purchase and delivery to you of merchandise, and the time it takes to receive and fulfil orders.

If these five rules are obeyed a good deal of junk mail can be avoided. Whether or not it is junk mail will be the decision of the receiver. Junk mail is rather like the garden weed, which is a plant which is where it shouldn't be, even if it's an orchid. Most of the 'weeds' which make our gardens untidy are delightful 'wild flowers' when growing in the countryside. Thus, what is junk mail for some is a pleasure and a benefit for others. Can you work out who are the unwanted 'some' and who are the desirable 'others'?

2 Three secrets of successful direct response marketing

The three essentials of successful direct response marketing are:

1 A good offer.
2 A good mail shot.
3 A good mailing list.

Lester Wunderman has reversed this order by saying that the *list* followed by the *offer* are the two most vital variables in direct response marketing. Today, the development of in-house customer or outside specialized databases has contributed enormously to the efficiency of the mailing list. That is, provided there is rigorous control. Lists need to be culled and corrected regularly and not allowed to accumulate indiscriminately. Inefficient databases or misuse of them can also contribute to junk mail.

Returning to the three essentials in the order given above, let us consider the importance of the *offer*.

A GOOD OFFER

A good offer depends on two things: skill in buying the right merchandise at the right price, and skill in packaging a proposition and knowing what the market is likely to buy. The two go together. Do you know your customers' needs, do you judge by the take-up of previous offers, or do you research the market?

Research can take many simple forms, and the following are some suggestions:

1 You can do a sample mailing, either to a sample of your mailing list or in a particular area which contains typical

buyers. This is a kind of test marketing. By setting a desired percentage of acceptances you can test whether this is achieved. If that percentage is achieved or bettered you can undertake the broad-scale marketing. If the result is a flop you can drop the idea and try something else. This sort of testing can also be done with mail shots themselves, or prices, to arrive at the one most likely to succeed. Sometimes it is not the merchandise which is right or wrong: it can be your presentation of the offer, or the price. There are psychological attitudes to price, so that a small difference in price can make an offer more or less acceptable. This can be more subtle than the familiar £99 or £19.99. Research can show whether 48p sells better than 52p, or whether postage should be included or added on.

2   You can study what is currently available in the shops or on the market. Is something obviously popular and in demand, which you can supply? Conversely, is something unavailable, can something fill an obvious want? Think back at some of the novel things now on offer which no one was previously supplying: holidays for singles or the elderly; insurance against loss of credit cards or keys; exclusive fashions; and, years ago, first-day covers.

3   Other people's offers are worth analysing to see whether you can offer something different, better or cheaper.

4   Visits to exhibitions and trade fairs, in the UK and abroad, may reveal merchandise which you can handle.

5   Trade magazines, in their editorials and advertisements, may suggest goods, manufacturers or importers which can be useful to you.

6   Foreign countries, anxious to export to your country, frequently hold trade shows, or have trade centres, where you can view products which may not be normally available in the shops.

One way and another, by keeping your eyes open, and by exploiting opportunities, you can find or create original, interesting offers of value to your customers and profit to you.

Be explicit
Armchair shopping does mean that prospective customers

virtually have the shop brought into their living room. They should be given almost as much information as they would get in a retail shop or from a visiting salesman. Their confidence relies on this. They will not thank you for bamboozling them with misleading information. Doubts must not emerge because your wording or illustrations are inadequate and unconvincing.

It pays to analyse exactly what information the recipient of your mailing is likely to need. They probably won't go to the trouble of writing to you or phoning you about details you have omitted.

This is not easy to accomplish because you know all about the merchandise or service, whereas the recipient has never heard of it before the arrival of your mail shot. Bridging this communication gap is a skill you have to learn. Make sure you have given all the facts and explanations the reader needs to know in order to understand your offer.

The key to this is often *keep it simple*. One way to bewilder a prospect is to spread the message over many pieces of paper instead of presenting the essential message in a compact, simple-to-understand format. Sometimes an envelope can be full of so many items that the reader does not know which bit to look at first and in desperation discards the lot. Why do so many mailings have such a superfluity of loose paper?

For instance, twice in one year the Automobile Association offered its members a Profit Plus Plan linked with the Scottish Life Assurance Company, inviting monthly investments in a unit trust fund. There were *eight* pieces of paper of various sizes plus a business reply envelope. They consisted of:

A long letter on AA Insurance heading, printed on both sides of two odd-shaped unattached sheets. It really repeated everything said elsewhere, except that it lacked certain vital information.

A large three-colour proposal form which purported to answer all your questions, but didn't.

A six-page two-colour folder on 'How to earn more from your savings', which was repetitive save for an example of investment growth and a history of Scottish Life.

A small full-colour leaflet offering two gifts.
A black and white leaflet about a bonus, which again was repetitive.
A red leaflet about a lump sum investment.
A small two-colour folder on the accumulator offer.
A two-page black and yellow memorandum which was yet again repetitive, with the free gifts repeated on the back.

One can only ask why was there this plethora of repetitive information in different shapes and forms? It was all in the four-page letter, which need only have been accompanied by a more simple proposal form.

The investment was to be put in the Scottish Life Management Fund, the value of units being given in the *Financial Times* or the *Daily Telegraph* if one happened to be a reader. They were not listed in the unit trusts prices printed in the *Guardian* or *The Independent*, or in the performance assessment listings in *Money Observer*. What sort of fund was it? How big was it? Why did so many papers fail to list it? What sort of gilts or equities, UK or foreign stocks and shares was your money likely to be invested in? Why this lack of essential information?

The strength of the offer lay in its flexibility, no requirement for a medical examination, and an age limit of 75. Unlike other schemes, no number of years was specified, although £1000 had to remain if withdrawals were made. But for how long did the scheme continue? For ever, apparently! The offer was extremely vague on this point. For how long did this basic £1000 or the whole investment have to remain? There was a reference to 'the first ten years' – but supposing one started the scheme aged 75! It was all very, very vague, and it was possible for people to invest in the scheme with very little understanding of *how* their money was going to be invested or for *how long* they were committed!

So here was a case of a scheme which may well have been splendid, except that it was not fully explained, and was either inefficiently conceived or was exploiting inadequate information – and lacked credibility to anyone who did buy insurance, unit trusts or shares.

Mr Wunderman's mailing list – in this case the membership

list of the AA presumably – may well be excellent, but everything starts with the offer. If that is faulty, the most perfect mailing list is merely a way of subsidizing the Post Office. The quality and appropriateness of the offer must come first.

A GOOD MAIL SHOT

This second secret of success needs careful thought and precise planning. In succeeding chapters a variety of elements of a mail shot are discussed – sales letter, one-piece mailers, envelopes, insertions, gimmicks and catalogues. The choice is so wide that it is easy to be dazzled by the cleverness of some of the options.

Your choice lies largely in your understanding of the psychology of your recipient. Shall it be a great four-colour broadsheet or a simple sales letter? And how shall it be packaged – what sort of envelope shall be used? The basic principles to apply include the following, but your kind of business may suggest others.

Acceptability
What sort of mail shot is most likely to be well received? Receiving mail is often a pleasure, so don't abuse this initial advantage that direct mail has over any other advertising medium. The junk mailers fail to enjoy this basic privilege.

For instance, if you are planning a holiday and have applied for a brochure, the fun of planning a holiday is enhanced when a printed envelope arrives announcing that it is what you have been eagerly expecting. Even in a commercial office this anticipation can be satisfied when the secretary sees that the envelope contains something for which the boss is waiting.

But even if the mailing is unsolicited it can be welcomed if it promises something interesting and useful. Remember Dr Johnson's famous words that advertising is all promise, great promise.

Relevance
Is the mail shot relevant to the needs of the potential customer?

This may depend very much on the selectivity of the mailing list, but even then is the offer relevant to the chosen recipients? This needs thinking about. When an insurance company mails newly-weds, or people recently promoted, the offer can be very relevant. The same can apply if a local store mails all the residents of a new housing estate. The owners of houses with large gardens obviously own lawnmowers, and it will be relevant to mail them in the spring and autumn about servicing their machines.

Credibility
Is the offer convincing, either about the benefits of the offer, or your ability to give satisfaction? Remember, although you may have been in business a long time, there are people who have never heard of you. It is easy to have a good mirror image of yourself, whereas the perceived image held by outsiders can be very different!

Therefore it is important that the mail shot establishes a clear corporate image. You need to make it clear who you are, what you do, how reliable you are and so on. This may be done by explaining your history, quoting genuine testimonials, giving facts and figures where appropriate, and offering any applicable guarantees or promises of replacements or refunds. Some mail order traders invite customers to visit showrooms.

Although some criticisms were made above about the AA/ Scottish Life scheme, it did have two strengths concerning corporate image. The AA has a sound reputation with its members – its many services including motor insurance brokerage are excellent – and a description was given of Scottish Life's 100-year history, its £1300m assets, and its 'mutual' ownership by policyholders.

The corporate image can be created by the kinds of merchandise or services you offer, or by the reputation you have built up over the years, or by the style of your mail shot.

The styling of mail shots is therefore important in its effect on your corporate image. Does it suggest that you are reputable and enterprising, or that you are too pushy and too clever by half? For these reasons the various methods and devices described in later chapters must be considered very carefully as they apply to your kind of business and your kind of customers.

The credibility factor is often ignored in the craze for cleverness. Direct response marketing has certainly grown, but it is full of cowboys who are destroying its credibility through the overuse of gimmicks. The trouble with some of these gimmicks is that they have lost the originality they once had twenty or thirty years ago when introduced by, say, *Reader's Digest*. Copied today by new but very big entrants into direct response marketing, they have sometimes become silly and the novelty has palled. You can judge for yourself by what arrives in your own mail.

The only excuse, perhaps, is that new uses of old ideas are made in appeals to people lower down the social grades who may be persuaded by these methods. It is also true that the most successful word in advertising is 'free', but this should be used legitimately, and successful more recent uses are in Freepost and Freefone. But this magic appeal can be abused, and when applied to more serious or costly products and services there is the risk of overkill which destroys credibility.

For example, what is one to make of the following from Holiday Exchange Network of London?

Dear Mrs . . .

IMPORTANT – IMMEDIATE RESPONSE REQUIRED

I am delighted to tell you that you have been selected to receive one of several valuable awards listed below:

CATEGORY A	CATEGORY B	CATEGORY C
Microwave Oven	Clock Radio w/Cassette	Video Recorder
35 mm Camera w/Flash	3 Piece Luggage Set	£300 Cash
£150 Cash	14″ Colour Television	Home Burglar Alarm

Your award is determined by the code shown above and will be issued to you at our Award Centre by matching the above number against our master list.

To **FIND OUT WHICH AWARD CATEGORY YOU** are selected to **RECEIVE** call me **TODAY** on 01–235–8020 between 9.00 a.m. and 7.00 p.m. (Monday to Saturday) and I will also make an appointment for you to tour our Award Centre and claim your award.

CALL US BETWEEN 9.00 A.M. AND 7.00 P.M. TODAY
on 01–235 8020 AND ASK FOR LISA
FIND OUT WHICH AWARD CATEGORY YOU
ARE TO RECEIVE

Call us now. Your award is awaiting your collection.

Yours sincerely,

Lisa Tate
Award Liaison Manager

The way in which the letter was addressed revealed that 'You have been selected' probably meant 'as one of the millions who bought British Gas shares'. Nowhere in the letter does it say what is being sold. It is only when one reads the information on the back that one finds it is a time share promotion and that participation is dependent on certain employment, income and marital conditions. The implication is that the recipient is guaranteed one of the nine awards. Is this plausible, except to the gullible? Credibility is stretched beyond belief. Except, of course, that the conditions limited the number of participants to those interested in time share.

Sun Alliance have followed the familiar routine by sending an advance letter warning recipients of their impending good fortune – another gimmick which is no longer fresh. Always, recipients are addressed as the chosen few. As one Sun Alliance advance letter heralded: 'I am very pleased to inform you that you are among those selected. . . .' One can imagine the labels pouring out of the computer printer. It is the usual lie. The letter went on:

Before too long an envelope from Sun Alliance – clearly marked '£38,750 Special Invitation Prize Draw – 228 Cash

Prizes must be won!' – should arrive at your address.

It was better than that – or was it a misorganized coincidence that another envelope from the Sun Alliance arrived by the same post? It was sheer luck which envelope got opened first. More funny words formed a PS to the advance letter:

On behalf of all my colleagues at Sun Alliance, may I also recommend that you act promptly to take full advantage of all the opportunities it brings you.

The daftness of this pretentious nonsense is apparent when it is realized that the mailing list did not consist of obscure British Gas shareholders, but actual policyholders!

The two-page sales letter used for the second mailing, which coincided with the advance letter, was written in terrible tax inspector vocabulary; it did not mention the prize draw but offered a choice of four free gifts. Very confusing. Why is it necessary to offer a free gift to sell an insurance-linked savings scheme? It was really another version of the AA/Scottish Life offer, but with immediate life cover. And there were the inevitable bits of coloured paper in various shapes and sizes.

Both letters were signed by the same manager, but one was addressed to the husband and one to the wife! This double cock-up did not inspire credibility. It was another appalling example of junk mail. Poor Mr Graham J. Treharne, Manager, Life Division of Sun Alliance: the things that are written and done in your name by whoever bungles your direct response operation!

You may have realized by now that Sun Alliance were conducting two entirely different direct response marketing schemes, each having free gift incentives, which were despatched simultaneously, either to the same or different mailing lists!

Unfortunately you are at the mercy of the big spenders in this game, who are incredibly clumsy, capable of alienating your market, and producers of a high volume of junk mail. So, study what you yourself receive, analyse it and learn from it.

A GOOD MAILING LIST

A good offer and a good mail shot will fail or succeed according to the quality of the mailing list. This can be the most critical and difficult aspect of direct response marketing using direct mail.

The great advantage of direct mail is the ability to select prospects, and to appeal to them directly and personally at their addresses, compared with the more hit-or-miss broadcast effect of the mass media. Ideally, that should mean that it is both more economic and more effective than press, radio, TV or posters.

Unfortunately, the very strengths of direct mail can be weakened if there are faults in the mailing system, as the derogatory expression 'junk mail' implies. The third secret of success lies in how efficiently you conduct your mailing. This will be dealt with more thoroughly in a separate chapter, but here let us consider the hazards regarding lists.

If directories or membership lists are used, unless they are produced from last-minute computerized entries like the *Hollis Press and Public Relations Annual*, they are bound to be slightly out of date when published because addresses are constantly changing.

Professional people often belong to more than one society or institute and it may be difficult to avoid repeat mailings.

It may not be easy to de-duplicate lists which are computerized because a search may not locate variations in names. This problem is intensified when wrong spellings have been keyed in originally. When numerous errors occur – as with a name like mine! – it may be impossible to locate duplications, and multiple mailings will occur. Irritated recipients may complain, only to find that their complaints have been ignored because the errors are repeated in the future. People are very vain about the correct spelling of their names. To maintain good relations it pays to try to make corrections, but this may not be possible if you are using someone else's database or list and you have no direct access to it.

One way of keeping lists *alive* is to send postcards to past recipients asking whether they still wish to be mailed. Lists based on coupon responses can accumulate prodigiously. Postcard checks are made by book publishers and horticultural firms. They save wasteful expenditure on mailing expensive catalogues to people no longer interested, alive or still living at the same address. Non-replies can be eliminated. This is not always done, as new residents find when they receive mail – sometimes for years! – addressed to former residents. *The validity of most mailing lists is rarely more than six months.*

When using list brokers or databases it is worth asking what is the age of their lists, or how well they update them. Think how frequently share registers change, and how difficult it has been to locate people due to pay instalments in some of the privatization share issues. Hundreds of Premium Bond winners have gone missing. People are very lax about reporting changes of address, and in your case there is often no reason why they should inform you. Lists also become out of date because people die, go abroad, change jobs or marry and change their names. The recency of a list is therefore important. Some wastage is inevitable, but it can be minimized.

FREQUENCY OF MAILINGS

The right frequency of mailings is a key decision which you should make right at the start. Some propositions can be made only once, others should be followed up, while periodic reminders may be desirable. Or you may make sequential mailings of different offers. Regular mailings have the merit of repetition, and they establish the permancy of your business. Only you can prevent people from forgetting you. Repetition is a major device in most advertising.

One-off offers, follow-ups, reminders and regular mailings are strategies you must adopt as appropriate to your business.

One engineering company bored its trade customers by sending out a monthly sales letter of incredible dullness. If it is necessary to mail as frequently as that, make sure that each shot contains an interesting and valuable proposition. It helps if there is a welcome on the mat because the recipient enjoys and benefits from your mailings. For instance, a stamp collector will welcome news of new issues from a philatelic dealer just as a member of a book or record club will welcome the quarterly magazine containing new titles.

If a series is used, each succeeding letter should avoid making recipients feel they have been impolite in not responding to the previous one. It can present a new angle on the same subject. A series from a dry cleaner can be topical about the items which should be cleaned each month. Similarly, a department store can offer topical or seasonal goods in a series of mailings. Series should be sent at reasonable intervals, such as monthly or quarterly.

Reminders are not always the same as series. It has been found that identical repeat mailings can be successful with the words 'reminder' overprinted on the envelope or letter. This may seem a lazy sort of reminder, but there are always people who for one reason or another mislaid or never saw the original mailing, or forgot to respond to it.

Reminders can also be made in the future, following up either enquiries or regular customers when the subject is topical again. Examples include motor-car or household insurance, annual servicing of equipment, holidays, or optical services.

But care should be taken to make sure that reminders have not been sent to people who have already responded and made purchases. This would seem to be an elementary precaution, and so would the keeping of records of responses. American Express are constant culprits; they do not seem to know who are their cardholders, and they repeatedly mail existing cardholders with invitations to apply for an American Express card. Similarly, Norwich Union invited investments in their Asset Management managed fund, and then some months later mailed reminders to people who had already invested £1500 and more. With such substantial investments you would have thought they knew who their policyholders were!

Follow-ups are often well worth the trouble, provided they are tactful and pursue the sales offer with additional information or perhaps a new inducement. But be careful not to fall into the trap of encouraging people to expect that if they wait long enough there will be a worthwhile price reduction. This ploy of offering a set of reducing prices with succeeding follow-ups is used a great deal by correspondence schools, and students learned to wait for the 'final' offer. It is rather like the bazaar salesman with his 'last price'.

But failure to follow up can be a sacrifice of potential business once the doubts and inertia have been overcome. If you are using your own database it is easy to run a file of enquiries over a certain period for which the computer will search and print out labels. This can be done on the simplest of personal computers such as an Amstrad, which may be ideal for the smaller business.

IN-HOUSE OR DIRECT MAIL HOUSE?

Should you run your own direct response unit, or should you employ a direct mail house? Much will depend on whether the size of your operation warrants expenditure on equipment, whether you have your own database of customers and enquiries, or whether you need outside advice, creative services, the benefit of despatch equipment and access to lists. Large and small firms do it themselves, but there are also numerous specialist direct mail agencies which service clients of all sizes. In between are owners of databases and list brokers. More will be said about the latter in Chapter 4 on mailing lists. Here, let us consider the pros and cons of the in-house unit and the direct mail house.

In-house direct response unit
Advantages
1   You have complete and instant control over the whole operation, including purchase of merchandise, creation of mail shots, compilation of the mailing list, despatch of mailings, and recording of enquiries/sales.
2   You can produce your own mailing lists more critically and selectively, and with less risk of duplication or error.
3   You can use a personal computer to record the history of an enquiry, follow-up, sale or whatever sequence of information you wish to store. This can be used for future

mailings, and a store of filters can be built up to select addresses for label printing.

4   You have absolute control over the timing of mailings, which may be critical with urgent or dated offers for which there is a need to move stock quickly. You may want to solve a cash flow problem! Or you may want to clear stock which is the end of a line, has suffered a price change, or has become obsolete.

5   You may want to make specialist offers to short mailing lists.

6   You may also want to make follow-ups to enquiries which have not converted to sales, or customers who are late payers of instalments.

In other words, with your own unit you have better control, you can be more flexible, and you can introduce various submailings.

Disadvantages

1   You need to be creative, and capable of writing sales letters or other mailing pieces.

2   You need to be able to prepare material for print, and work with printers. This will involve layouts and artwork, and the giving of typographical instructions.

3   You need to be able to buy material such as letterheadings, artwork, photography and envelopes, and to know their sources.

4   You need to understand postal facilities and be able to work with your area postal sales representative.

5   You may need to buy equipment to reproduce, fold, insert and frank mailings – but this will depend on the volume of work.

6   You need the means and the time to sort mail in order to enjoy Post Office rebates.

If you lack creative abilities you can use freelance services or a local studio.

Direct mail house

1   It is set up specially to handle everything creative and

physical. This will include writers, artists, buyers and equipment.

2 It can offer professional advice on how to devise a direct marketing scheme suitable for your business.

3 It has a pool of experience gained from handling campaigns for a variety of other clients.

4 You can virtually share creative and mechanical facilities which are uneconomical to employ full time if you are not making large or frequent mailings.

5 It will be familiar with sources of material to use in mailings, including envelope makers and printers, or suppliers of gifts and incentives.

Checklist for choosing a mailing house

1 Are they familiar with your kind of work? Pay them a visit and find out.

2 What equipment do they have for reproducing, addressing, folding, filling, sealing, sorting and franking?

3 What are their relations with postal and other despatch services, such as local Post Office representative, local TNT representative (of overseas mail), door-to-door distributors (including free newspaper distributors), or other means of delivery? Can they organize prompt, correctly timed, and the most economic despatch?

4 Do they offer fulfilment services, or are they associated with a fulfilment house, for the handling of coupons, sales promotion offers or orders?

5 Do they offer a 24-hour service?

6 Who are their envelope suppliers/printers, and what variety of envelopes or overprinted designs do they offer? Do they offer shrinkwrapping, which you need when mailing a catalogue or display pack?

7 Is their location convenient for you to supply material? You may prepare or have produced mail shots independently and only require mailing facilities.

8 What are their list facilities, including computerizing and maintaining your own (perhaps on-line), working with list brokers or databases, and using geographic-

demographic systems such as ACORN or PIN? (These systems are explained in Chapter 4.)

9 What creative services do they offer? Do they have their own writers, photographers and studio, or do they use freelances and outside services?
10 Do they offer an advisory service? Will they plan campaigns for you?
11 What have they done for other clients? It will be worth studying examples of their work.
12 Do they service any of your rivals? Confidentiality may be necessary for security reasons in this highly competitive business.
13 Have they won any awards, such as those of the British Direct Marketing Association, the Post Office, the Institute of Sales Promotion, or the American Direct Marketing Association?
14 What are their charges? These should be quoted for every operation.

The names and addresses of mailing houses will be found in *Direct Response*, in other journals like *Campaign* and *Marketing* which run direct marketing features, and in directories like *Advertiser's Annual*. The addresses of these publications are given in the Bibliography.

3   How to write sales letters

Sales letters! Receivers of direct mail often feel they are being pestered with a flood of questions and propositions. They remind you of that picture of the boy being harangued by the Roundhead officer: 'When did you last see your father?'

The writing of sales letters is one of the most highly skilled forms of copywriting. A sales letter is not just a business letter. It is an advertisement. But nor is it a sales leaflet topped and tailed with 'Dear Sir/Madam' and 'Yours faithfully'.

Look more carefully at all those sales letters you receive – before you throw them away. Why do you throw them away? Because they are dreadful! Or they are irrelevant.

Why are they dreadful? For some of the following seven reasons.

They are too long

Sales letter writers often suffer from the proverbial verbosity of salesmen. Perhaps they are written by sales managers who just do not know when to stop dictating. They do not compose creatively, boiling it down and down until they have conveyed the fullest message in the fewest number of words.

Some letters spread over two, four, even six pages. *One page should be enough.* Psychologically, sight of the signature at the foot of the page encourages you to read. An obvious continuation is discouraging. Why make a letter off-putting before it is read?

Perhaps we should be warned by the fact that mail order is now called direct response *marketing.* Marketing people tend to go in for a lot of words. Maybe the *marketing* influence is not healthy for direct mail. Marketing people can convert a crisp, factual, newsy press release into pages of unpublishable drivel.

It was way back in 1977 that David Ogilvy, in his keynote speech to the first Direct Marketing Day, said 'If anyone tells you that long letters don't sell, he doesn't know anything about direct mail.' It was possible to say that if the proposition was of sufficient interest and if it was directed at the right prospects, a long sales letter could then be justified. But the whole direct marketing scene has changed since Ogilvy's speech.

The sales letter often has to compete for attention with enclosures; databases have made available new and sometimes very broad-based lists (such as share registers); and the sheer quantity of mail shots going out has created competition for reading time. The day has passed when a recipient only occasionally received a direct mail shot, and could spend time absorbing a long sales letter.

Today, a short sales letter is more likely to be read. You can judge them for yourself if you are the receiver of a lot of direct mail. Which ones do you read, if you read them at all: the short or the long sales letters? It makes sense to aim to get read.

They don't look like letters
Surely if one is writing a letter it should look like a letter. Yet many so-called sales letters resemble sales leaflets. Some are more like newsletters. They are four- or six-page folders, printed on both sides. Why on *both* sides? You wouldn't type a letter on both sides of your letterheading, would you?

The type is too small
Some letters are miniaturized to get a lot of words on the sheet. Once again, they don't look like letters. They lack credibility.

The personalization is overdone
Laser printing is very irritating when your name keeps appearing throughout the text of a letter. It is courteous to personalize the salutation, but enough is enough.

They are tedious and dull
Letter writing is an art. A letter should be pleasant to read. This is achieved by style, but especially by use of a varied

vocabulary, by a good mixture of different but apt words – like using a variety of notes in a piece of music. A good test is to read a letter aloud.

Readable letters are achieved by working on the draft, changing words, shortening sentences, using punctuation. Synonyms have to be sought, if necessary using a thesaurus. Sentences can be turned round, paraphrased. It may pay to start sentences with 'And' or 'But' to gain emphasis. You can have a one-word or one-sentence paragraph. It can be made conversational by using the vernacular, such as 'don't', 'wouldn't' or 'won't'. In fact, the nearer a letter sounds like someone *talking*, the more natural, personal and friendly it becomes. A letter should read like a message from one person to another.

But some sales letters are pompous and pretentious: 'I am pleased to inform you' sounds as if your divorce has come through or someone has found your lost cat.

A well-written sales letter immediately wins the reader's interest and attention, and if it has pace the reader will be carried along. This does not mean that it has to be over-exuberant, but the words do have to smile and please like a good tune. The rhythm of the writing can help this. The variety of short and longer sentences can help too. A letter has to resemble a sports car, not a steamroller.

Short paragraphs – with indentations where white space leads the eye in again and again – can help the reader to read on.

That's another point. The block paragraphs of typical business letters do not encourage reading. You would not want to read a book or a newspaper that did not have indented paragraphs. So why not use them in a sales letter and make it more readable?

There is overkill
Credibility is lost when a letter becomes too strident. The trouble with some sales letters is that they try too hard. You don't have to scream at people with underlinings, bold type, capital letters or colours. These devices are fine in a press advertisement, a sales leaflet or a catalogue, but a letter should be a letter.

Charity appeals have to appeal to the emotions, and this is done admirably in some of the very skilfully written press advertisements. An appeal from the NSPCC had a headline filling a third of a page in green underlined script, which read:

Will you give £20 this Christmas to help save a child's life?

The first paragraph read:

Dear Friend,
    That may sound dramatic but, in this country, on average three to four children a week die following abuse or neglect at the hands of their parents or guardians.

Let's analyse the letter further. The above is a good, compelling opening paragraph, but the underlining was unnecessary. The rest of the letter ran to four pages on two sheets, using both sides of the sheet. Nice, crisp short paragraphs were used, but the letter was far too long. Interspersed on unnumbered pages 2 and 3 were photographs, which meant that the wording alongside had to be reduced to half column width. The flow of the reading was unsettled by this device.

On three pages, underlined words were also given a green Stabilo felt-tip pen effect. Four of these had big green crosses in the left-hand margin. All this fussy over-emphasis detracted rather than attracted interest. There was then a PS in typewriter script, followed by a PPS in imitation handwriting, followed by a boxed message about reporting child abuse to the NSPCC. The writer simply could not let go.

Are any postscripts necessary? There is a school of thought in direct mail which says they are, but it is a rather amateur schoolgirlish device.

As if that was not more than enough, there was 'a brief note' from the director, two pages of reproduced press cuttings, a donation form bearing yet another letter from a *third* person, and a Freepost reply envelope. On top of that, the mailing list was so duplicated that more than one person in the same household received the same mailing.

Reaction to this hysteria? If they can afford to waste money like this they don't need *my* money! This was a pity because the NSPCC is a deserving cause, but potential donors are likely to resent being bludgeoned so hysterically and so wastefully. They didn't get my money, and I do respond to charity appeals. But it did win an industry award!

Another problem with charity appeals is that if you are a regular donor to charities your name gets on lists which appear to be sold to other charities, and you are inundated by numerous appeals week in, week out. The annoyance and wastage factors must be great, but this folly is intensified when the appeal letters are written and designed with such an air of desperation.

They lack sincerity and therefore lose credibility
Some sales letters are too effusive or pretentious. Even the salutation may be too pally for a letter coming from a stranger. A common bit of insincerity is the delight or pleasure which some writers express, as in this example:

Dear Householder,
I am delighted to welcome you to the new improved facilities and wider range of services now available from your local branch of the Cheltenham & Gloucester Building Society at 26 George Street, Croydon.

It is not a bad opening sentence otherwise, but 'I am delighted' is hackneyed, cloying and unbelievable. Further examples will be found later in this chapter. Why is everyone so *pleased* and *delighted*? This is the most amateur, boring and stupid way to start a sales letter. Why should *he* be so pleased? There would be more sense in saying *you* will be delighted or pleased. The 'pleasure' is the wrong way round!

FOUR-POINT SALES LETTER FORMULA

Having reviewed these seven negative aspects, what are the *positive* aspects of a good sales letter? A proper format needs to be determined before writing anything, otherwise the letter degenerates into the turgid monstrosity which so frequently pretends to be a sales letter. It needs to be planned and have a clear progression of information. It needs a basic skeleton or synopsis, such as a professional writer prepares for a book, play, poem, article or even a news release.

Such a format imposes a discipline on the writer. This plot can take many shapes, and you may decide on one which suits you best. You may decide to blurt out your proposition right away, or introduce it in a more subtle manner. A lot of questions might first be posed, leading up to your solution as the proposition. However, here is a simple four-point formula which will be discussed stage by stage:

1   Attention-getting opening paragraph.
2   Interesting proposition.
3   Convincing sales argument.
4   Action-prompting closing paragraph.

Attention-getting opening paragraph
Preceding the first paragraph, should there be a headline? It may be used for emphasis, as an introduction, or a bold give-away of the offer. Or you may prefer to go straight into the letter. Here are some examples of the use of a headline.

The first is a follow-up from TSB Insurance Services Ltd to people who enquired about motor insurance, but failed to insure with the company. It is a pleasant, cheerful approach.

LAST YEAR YOU PASSED OUR SAFE DRIVER TICK
TEST. THIS YEAR, PICK UP YOUR REWARDS IF
YOU STILL QUALIFY

Dear Mr . . .
Cast your mind back to about a year ago. For it was around this time last year that you successfully completed our safe driver tick test and returned it to me.

The next one had an interesting offer of the *London Review of Books*, but it was neither a sales letter nor a sales leaflet because typewriter-style paragraphs had large subheadings in a different typeface and in blue. The opening paragraph is pretentious with its 'I'm delighted'. Why do people use these wretched 'pleased to tell you' approaches, which sound so insincere? However, here is another example of the use of a headline, this time in testimonial style:

As Clive James says, 'When a paper is as good as this one, it hurts to throw old copies away.'

Dear Reader,

I'm delighted to introduce you to the *London Review of Books* and to have the opportunity of giving you a taste of the pleasure it contains.

The letter went on as a four-page folder. It went on and on. Now for three examples of which none uses a headline but each has a very different quality. The first is from the Bradford Exchange, offering a collectible; the second is from the Inter-Continental Hotels about their Rewards scheme; and the third is from the Institute of Marketing, from whom one might have expected something better.

Dear Friend,

Suppose that twenty-five years ago the Chairman of IBM had offered you stock in his company, and guaranteed to buy it back any time during the first year for the full price you paid.

Dear Mr . . .

We know our guests expect the extraordinary from us. So when we decided to put together a program for our frequent guests, we knew that it too had to be extraordinary.

Dear Client

Prospectus 1988

I am pleased to send you our latest Prospectus of public courses for 1988. As before, you will find a comprehensive range of courses developed to help improve the performance of people employed in a marketing function in all aspects of their job, and to help non-marketers at all levels understand marketing.

They may sound like isolated appeals, but all five of these examples were addressed to the same people who happened to recur in five different mailing lists. This is also an example of how, nowadays, the same person can receive a lot of direct mail. Such a person can be a motorist, a book reader, a collector, a traveller and someone interested in training. It's interesting how a mere name on a mailing list can play a variety of roles, and this role-playing characteristic of the recipient is a guide to how a sales letter should be written.

Consequently, the different approaches made in these opening paragraphs may or may not be the correct or best one. For instance, is the Institute of Marketing's opening paragraph too stolid (forgetting for a moment the 'I am pleased'), or should it be this serious? Should the Inter-Continental Hotel example be so exuberant, or is that to be expected?

The essential thing is to use an opening that will get the rest of the letter read. It can be anecdotal like that of the Bradford Exchange, or nicely timed, light-hearted and helpful like that of the TSB.

Now let us look at the five salutations. Only two were personalized; the others used 'Dear Reader', 'Dear Friend' and 'Dear Client'. While 'Dear Reader' is apt, 'Dear Friend' is a bit presumptuous, and 'Dear Client' is rather odd as well as being cold. Never say 'Dear Sir/Madam'. 'The Occupier' is even worse. Overall, the Institute of Marketing effort is somewhat clumsy and unimaginative.

One way of claiming attention is to pose a question – but you have to be careful not to provoke a negative response which ends the reader's interest. Here is an interesting one from a subscription renewal letter sent out by *South* magazine. It aims to overcome the problem of maintaining subscriptions or recapturing interest. It is so easy not to renew a subscription by either default or cessation of interest.

Dear Subscriber,
Do you, like most people, groan when a renewal notice comes through your door? Do you sigh and think – 'Is it already renewal time?'

The letter went on to remind the subscriber of current world affairs and of the magazine's global perspective. But it went on too long, using subheadings in blue, and filling two pages printed on both sides of the sheet. You can try too hard.

The writing of the opening paragraph is going to make or break the letter, and you may find that you will have to rewrite it many times to get it right. The opening paragraph in most types of writing is often the most difficult part of any literary exercise, whether it is a letter, a news release, a feature article, a book, a short story or an advertisement.

You may find it is best to write the first paragraph *last*, that is after the main copy has been written and you know what you want to lead into.

Interesting proposition

After the opening paragraph should come the proposition, and we have already discussed the choice of offer and its relevance to those on your mailing list. This may run over a number of paragraphs if necessary, being built up step by step to create interest and desire to buy.

Convincing sales argument

This may be implicit in the whole letter, or you may need to lead up to convincing reasons why a purchase should be made. Some of the reasons may be:

1 The price – a special price, a discount for quantity, or a discount for instant reply.
2 A timed offer.
3 An offer of a gift.
4 Testimonials or some proof of successful usage, such as a rise in value of investments, research tests, or use by quotable customers.
5 A guarantee, or promise of a refund if not satisfied.
6 The opportunity to view at a showroom.

And so on.

Action-prompting closing paragraph

A mail shot is static (unless you have an enclosure such as a scratch card), and yet it has to admonish the reader to do something. What do you want them to do? Here are some suggestions:

1 Fill in the order form and make payment.
2 Telephone the order.
3 Invite a salesman to call.
4 Visit your premises.
5 Complete a reply card for samples.

Whatever the action, it should be prompted by the last paragraph, and you should make it easy for the reader. It should never be too much trouble for the action to be taken. Telephone numbers with area codes or Freefone, business reply or Freepost cards or envelopes, location directions or maps, and clear instructions about payment including perhaps credit cards or direct debit facilities, should be carefully thought out to overcome any sort of inertia or sales resistance. Put yourself in your reader's mind. Consider his or her role-playing and its effect on decision-making. Like the first paragraph, this final salvo is vital to the success of the mailing. Ideally, the preceding paragraphs should have prepared the reader for action.

EXAMPLE OF A SALES LETTER

The following is an imaginary example of a letter which may be sent out during the autumn from a local garden centre. The mailing list can consist of women living in private houses, the addresses being taken from the electoral roll or postcodes but eliminating flat dwellers. The appeal is to pleasure, pride and perhaps vanity. The style is light and pleasant. It aims to make it easy for the customer to find the garden centre, and seeks to overcome any objection that the goods are a nuisance to carry.

Dear Gardener,
    Would you like people to admire your front garden next spring?
    You can do this quite easily and cheaply with an unusual display of the new Dutch Windmill tulips. And enjoy them yourself!
    Each tulip has four petals like a windmill. Each petal is a different colour, such as red, white, pink and yellow, but there are various bright colour variations.
    They are sturdy, they stand eight inches tall, and the blooms are long lasting, making a colourful show. Your front garden will be the envy of all your neighbours!
    If you plant them now you will have a wonderful display next May. And if you leave them in the ground they will

multiply and bloom year after year. Make sure you plant them three inches deep. That's all you have to do.

Our bulbs are top size and cost only £1 per dozen or £4 for 50.

You can collect your Dutch Windmill tulips now from the Garden Centre opposite the Post Office in the High Street.

Pick them up when you are next doing your shopping. They are conveniently packed for you in a carrier bag.

Yours faithfully

JOHN SMITH
Manager

A more serious letter can be sent by a local newspaper advertisement manager to local traders, and the following is another imaginary example. In a fairly short letter it tells the recipient some interesting things he may not have known.

Dear Mr . . .

Do you know what 90 000 people do on Fridays and over the weekend? They don't all go fishing or visit their in-laws or even play golf. They read the *Weekly Advertiser*. Many of them could be your customers.

Did you realize, with all the freesheets about, that so many people still buy their local newspaper? Actually, our ABC figure continues to rise, although we have not increased our advertisement rates.

The *Weekly Advertiser* usually lives in people's homes until the next issue comes out. Different members of the household refer to it throughout the week. Think how many times your advertisement can be seen by at least two if not three times the circulation figure. It's more like a quarter of a million people.

If you want to use illustrations, picture quality is perfected by our computerized scanner. You can have full colour if you wish. For paper set ads our computerized typesetters offer 50 different typefaces, so that your wording can have character and originality.

Your advertisement must reach us not later than noon Monday to appear in the same week's issue. Our rate card is enclosed. You may reserve space by telephone, or post or deliver your advertisement to this office.

If you would like to discuss the most profitable way to promote your business, you have only to phone and invite our representative to call.

Yours sincerely,

In the above example the admonition contains a number of options, so that without being pestered the recipient is offered service.

Finally, while charity appeals may arrive by every post, and many are either dreary or overpowering, the following letter from the Royal Commonwealth Society for the Blind is irresistible. At least, that was my response.

The Gift of Sight

Dear Mr Jefkins,

May I share with you a visit I made recently to the village of Gorai, near Dhaka, in Bangladesh. There I met Abdul the local weaver, creating his intricately patterned cloth on his wooden loom. Later that day, I was introduced to Zarina, who was preparing the evening meal in her brightly decorated hut. Outside, Mohsena her ten-year-old daughter was learning to read, write and thread a needle.

Weeks before, they were all blind . . . but then one of our medical teams, led by Doctor Hussain, conducted an 'eye camp' in their village. People came from miles around; tents became improvised wards; the school classroom was converted into a temporary operating theatre; and volunteers served hundreds of rice meals a day.

Ten days later, with the bandages removed, they opened their eyes to the first shock of light. In all, seventy-three blind villagers had their sight restored at that 'eye camp'. It seems a miracle, yet the cost to this Society was just £15 to perform these three operations for Abdul, Zarina and Mohsena.

During the last year, our medical teams have restored sight to 214 033 blind men, women and children. Yet, for each person in that multitude, sight came as an individual miracle. It was made possible because someone like you cared that a fellow human being might otherwise remain needlessly blind. No gift could have been more precious – but there remains so much still to do.

At this moment, in the impoverished countries where we work, there are nearly <u>seven million curably blind people.</u> After thirty-seven years of experience, our medical teams have a skill which, given the money, could restore sight to thousands more people during the next few months.

Will you invest in that skill? Will you spare £15 to give three people the incomparable gift of sight? . . . £160 would save the sight of a whole village in *your* eye camp.

Your help is desperately needed, but time is not on our side. Your generosity today will give sight, hope and independence tomorrow to people who must otherwise remain blind.

Yours sincerely,

Alan W Johns

PS   Please close your eyes for a moment, and imagine what it would be like never to see again. Your gift of £15 (the equivalent of £1.25p per month) will restore sight to three more people who are needlessly blind.

That is a gem of a letter. So interesting, sincere and compelling! No gimmicks. The only enclosures were useful ones: a donation form and a reply paid envelope.

4 How to compile and ensure good mailing lists

Today, there is no difficulty in finding or creating a good mailing list. There is a wealth of directories, list brokers and databases, and computers have made it easy to assemble in-house databases.

The problem is knowing how to select and use lists effectively and economically. The surfeit of addresses, even when rationalized by the geographic/demographic PIN, ACORN, MOSAIC and Royal Mail Consumer Location systems, invites profligate usage leading to duplication, irrelevant mailings and overmailings. This is nice for the Post Office, and it is no wonder that – in spite of appalling delivery services – the Post Office counts its profits in millions. Why subsidize the Post Office?

However, we must not be too unkind to the Post Office. As you will find in different chapters of this book, while obviously seeking to promote its own business – which is fair enough – it does offer a remarkable range of services which you can exploit to make your mailings more efficient.

A wealth of Post Office literature is available on all these services, and you are recommended to obtain a copy of the excellent Royal Mail *Guide to Effective Direct Mail*. This is a well-produced pictorial 32-page guide, and its emphasis is on the *quality* of direct mail. But when it speaks of the volume of direct mail having doubled in three years, you are entitled to question how much of that volume was really necessary.

I am a great believer in and a successful user of direct mail, but every week I fill half a dustbin with discarded mail shots. Many are thrown away because the sales letters are too long-winded, I am not in the market, the contents are too many, or I am simply warned by the printed envelopes not to open them.

If I had ever been a contestant on Ted Rogers' '3–2–1' TV programme I would have relished winning Dusty Bin.

Because I belong to several professional bodies, contribute to charities, have bought insurance, unit trusts or shares, and have certain interests and hobbies, my name and address (in numerous formats and incorrect versions) is on a whole library of mailing lists and databases. My experience is common. Direct marketing endures the irony that an otherwise excellent advertising medium is being abused by carelessness and overkill.

To make your use of direct mail effective, you need to select and control your mailing lists. It will save you a fortune and avoid alienating your market. Learn to be a miser over your mailings, and avoid blanket mailings. I know, for instance, that when I mail 4000 shots, some of my rivals mail 25 000. I know this because I am on their lists and receive up to six of their shots. You might ask why they bother to mail *me*!

Perhaps recipients of direct mail are the victims of a profitable form of exploitation which is not always in their interests. Almost any organization has some kind of list of members, enquirers, customers, donors and so on which can be useful to someone else. Simple membership lists of societies are easily used, and so are easily available lists like *Yellow Pages* and electoral rolls. 'I've got him on my list!' is the common cry of direct mail. But the sale of lists to list brokers, or the direct rental of one's list, is producing incomes of many thousands of pounds for some organizations. The origin of some lists can be detected from the styling of the address.

BUILDING YOUR OWN LIST

You may decide to build your own list. You can operate it yourself, and supply it to a list manager or to a direct mail house which will computerize it and use it for your mailings.

If you build your own list, you need to decide whether it is to be one which you will use more than once, either occasionally or frequently, or whether you will use it only once or at long intervals. This depends on the nature and size of your business.

For instance, if you are mailing a prospectus or list of events (such as courses, concerts or plays) it may pay to produce a new list each time, using whatever resources are up to date. For more frequent mailings you can have a live, accumulative list which you maintain regularly with deletions, additions and amendments.

It is fatal to just build an ever-accumulating list which is only added to but never changed. Quite a number of in-house lists are of this kind. They continue to contain non-responsive addresses, wrong addresses and others which no longer exist. This is the lazy man's way to build a mailing list, but it is common.

People often ring me and ask to be placed on my mailing list, and they are surprised when I tell them I do not keep one. That is not entirely true because my office is full of list sources, and some are computerized on a short-term basis. But for each mailing I initiate a relevant list from sources. This involves a considerable selection process, with the result that addressing, envelope, print, filling and postage costs are minimized. I am both mean and greedy, spending the least to get the most.

A problem with renting lists is that you may have no means of checking how well they are maintained by the original compiler. Database lists are probably more accurate because there are computer facilities for maintaining them, and the compilers may well be maintaining them for their own mailing purposes. But it is noticeable that lists that merely perpetuate reader enquiries to advertisements are often out of date after six months because such enquirers are never likely to notify changes in status, job or private addresses.

Here are some ways in which in-house lists (including databases) can be created, and you may be able to adopt some of these as they apply to your particular business.

SOURCES FOR IN-HOUSE LISTS

Customers
These can be classified by:

1 Sex
2 Age

3 Job title
4 Location
5 What they bought
6 Value of purchase
7 Method of payment:
    (a) Cash
    (b) Instalments
    (c) Credit
    (d) Credit card
8 Frequency of purchases
9 Date of last purchase
10 Department/branch bought from
or any other classification which may be applicable according
to whether you are a bookseller, printer, motor agent,
insurance broker, hotelier, service engineer, department store
manager and so on.

With the simplest personal computer, software can be
written to file this information, and it can be called up and
flagged as required for printing out labels and recording
follow-up. It can be done on an Amstrad, for example.

Directories and membership lists

Numerous UK and overseas trade directories are available,
and the membership lists of many societies can also be
obtained. Some are national, some local, and there are also
sources such as *Yellow Pages* and electoral rolls. It will pay to
buy these volumes each year.

But there is both an advantage and a disadvantage. Inevitably, the information in these books cannot be 100 per cent
up to date at the time of publication, and many changes of
address will occur as the year progresses. Not many publishers
issue quarterly updates like the *Hollis Press and Public Relations
Annual*, or have on-line current data like *Hollis*, but some do
offer update facilities. You may be able to correct such sources
by watching out for changes of address announcements in the
relevant trade press. This can be laborious, and you may have
to risk making some mistakes when using directories. If you
are using directories, it is wise to discard old editions and
invest in the latest, even if they cost £100 a copy.

Even so, if you keep your eyes open it is surprising how many up-to-date lists can be found in publications. For example, building societies are listed in *Money Observer*.

Membership lists have the weakness that they do not include the deletions and additions that occur after publication, although if you can obtain the society's newsletter or journal these changes can be found.

Newspapers, magazines, trade and professional journals

Additions or amendments to your mailing list can be made by subscribing to the journals relevant to your market. New appointments features can be useful. Personal notices of engagements and marriages may be another source. So can readers' letters. So, too, can be the marketing intelligence information and other listings of new companies, tenders and contracts which appear in journals like *Sales & Marketing Management*. It may pay to visit a good library and see what journals exist to which you can subscribe or apply to be placed on a controlled circulation mailing list.

Enquiries

Whether they be general enquiries by post or telephone, or in response to press advertising, they can be fed into the mailing list. However, you must use your discretion regarding their validity after a certain time. You may decide to eliminate all those which have not been converted to the customer file after, say, six months. This must be your decision according to your type of business and the type of enquirer. Students are unlikely to remain useful after they have passed their examinations, whereas gardeners may go on gardening all their lives. You must also be able to sense once-only buyers. Estate agents sometimes make the mistake of mailing people long after they have probably bought a house and moved.

Guarantee cards

If a person has purchased, say, a household appliance or a camera, and returned a guarantee card, it is likely that they will buy something else or an accessory. Here is a good source.

OTHER PEOPLE'S LISTS AND DATABASES

Many owners of lists are willing to rent them, and this can be a way of reaching specialist groups of prospects which you could not otherwise locate. Each month offers of such lists appear in *Direct Response* in the 'list helpline' feature, and for this reason it will be beneficial to invite the publishers to put you on their controlled circulation list. Some of the lists in 'List helpline' are highly specialized and quite unusual, for example:

Buyers of women's fashions
Professional people
Ex-public schoolboys
Correspondence school students
Academics
Caterers
Holiday brochure applicants
Purchasers of security equipment
Visitors to trade exhibitions
Buyers of chair covers

Lists can be managed by companies which have computer facilities for holding, updating and maintaining lists supplied by direct marketing clients. List brokers hold a variety of lists which they rent to clients. They have their own trade association, the British List Brokers Association (see Chapter 19) from whom information can be obtained. The list broker business amounts to nearly £8 million per year.

An example of a service for the capturing of databases is that offered by Valldata of Melksham. They take a client's information in any form and convert it into clean, accurate machine-readable format. All keyed data can be verified for accuracy. Output is made compatible with the client's computer, from IBM mainframe to microcomputer. Valldata can also convert from discette to computer standard magnetic tape or vice versa. The database is accessible for the production of labels, laser output, magnetic tapes, listings and other purposes, and databases from a thousand to more than a million have been captured by Valldata.

Numerous databases or megalists are available to direct marketers, and some will be demographic lists. They have been called the 'next generation of mailing lists'. They have evolved from the consumer lifestyle studies conducted in the USA by Leo Burnett in the 1970s, culminating in the Databank and the Behaviourbank. Databank was launched in 1985, was based on surveys conducted by Consumer Quest, and is included among the list rental services of the London company Listshop Ltd.

The newer Behaviourbank, offered in the UK by Mardev, is derived from the American Select & Save survey. In Britain, Mardev's system is based on a twice-yearly national shoppers survey conducted by Computerized Marketing Technologies using detailed psychographic and demographic questionnaires and offering a rollout quantity of two million households in 1988.

These 'value-added' lifestyle databases offer much more intimately defined lists than traditional groupings. The Mardev Behaviourbank rents lists selectable by:

Psychographic/family lifestyles
Credit card owners
Business/personal travel details
Investment/insurance ownership
Health/fitness interest
Outdoor activity interests
Sporting enthusiasts
Social and charity interests
Collectors
Fine food and wine interest
Types of electrical goods owned
Demographics
Home ownership
Type and length of residence
Marital status
Exact age of all adults
Presence and ages of children
Grandchildren
Income

Occupation
Working women
Types and numbers of car

The Listshop psychodemographic database is similar in breakdown. The company points out that consumers on their lists are highly responsive to direct mail since, when completing questionnaires identifying their characteristics and interests, they said they were mail responsive and wanted to receive special offers or mail that matched their interests. To a considerable extent these lists help to avoid junk mail, and to minimize wastage.

List and database management firms can offer 'merge/purge' services which combine lists while searching for duplications, inaccurate, incomplete or changed addresses. De-duplication procedures are also applied by checking postcodes as well as data such as date of birth, telephone or telex number. To do this, Inspectorate UCC Ltd use what they call their Tie Breaker device.

Pegasus, the *Reader's Digest* list management service, has its Postcode II system of postcoding 90 per cent or more of addresses on a client's unpostcoded file. The system also deals with misspelt streets and house names, and unreadable addresses. For non-IBM or smaller users there is an alternative on-line service for personal computer terminals.

These methods are dealt with very briefly here, but fuller information can be obtained from the companies whose addresses are listed at the end of the book. These and many other services are featured or advertised in journals such as *Direct Response*, *Marketing* and *Marketing Week*.

NET NAMES

The following is quoted from advice published by the British List Brokers Association, whose activities are described in Chapter 19.

Net names are effectively a discount system for volume users of third-party mailing lists.

List rental prices are generally non-negotiable, and as a user of lists you will be quoted the same price irrespective of whether you approach the list owner, the list manager or the broker about rental of a particular list.

However, if you intend to carry out a de-duplication exercise (merge/purge) prior to mailing, you may not physically mail *all* the names supplied on a particular list. This is because the same individuals may appear either on your own list or on two or more of the lists you are renting – and it is a wastage of print, production and postage costs, to say nothing of the annoyance factor, to mail any individual more than once in a particular mail shot.

History and experience have shown that after deduplication, you are likely to use in the region of 85 per cent of the names supplied. This quantity will, of course, vary depending on the numbers you are mailing, the size of your own list, and the accuracy with which you are targeting the third-party mailing lists.

However, this figure of 85 per cent has been identified as an industry norm and, as a result, many list owners, managers and brokers will offer an '85 per cent net names arrangement' on orders for list quantities of over 10 000 (or, in some cases, 20 000) names and addresses.

This means that you guarantee to pay full rental price for at least 85 per cent of the names supplied. If you only mail 75 or 80 per cent of the list, you will still be obliged to pay for 85 per cent. If you mail 90 or 95 per cent, you will be charged at full rental price for this percentage.

In addition, you will be required to cover the list owner's computer charges for the unused balance. These are known as 'running' or 'run-on' charges, and average £5–£10 per thousand names and addresses supplied.

Such 85 per cent net names arrangements are applied fairly freely in the UK consumer list market. Indeed, some list sources may give more favourable net name deals on very large quantity orders from a particular list. In the business-to-business sector, net name arrangements are less common and tend to apply only to the very large mailers. In the international sector, net names are largely unknown.

Even if you have agreed a net names percentage discount,

you will generally be invoiced initially for 100 per cent of the names supplied. This is later adjusted by means of credit notes once the computer bureau undertaking the de-duplication work has submitted proof of the final figures.

As standards and parameters between different computer bureaux vary substantially, it is recommended that you select a BLBA member company to undertake de-duplication work for you.

EXAMPLES OF DATABASES
OR MEGALISTS

EMAP Direct offers lists made up of readers of their ten computer and financial magazines such as *PC User*, *Minicomputer News* and *Money Week*. The lists are broken down geographically, by including classifications, job descriptions, equipment used, purchasing plans for the next twelve months, and computer applications. The *Money Week* list is broken down into 14 groups of financial intermediaries.

British Investors Database lists the 5 per cent of the population who control 60 per cent of the wealth, and covers 2.5 million households. Selection is by value and type of investments, family structure, age/occupation/area, Super Profile socio-economic groupings 1–36, and demographic clusters. This is the really naughty one, which actually boasts of having a database of first-time investors and investors in government issues. These are the people to blame for all those financial mailings that have littered the mat of everyman's castle since the Big Bang. No doubt only the Crash of 1987 put a curb on the fortunes of the waste-paper industry. More seriously, British Investors Database does offer 14 categories of investor, and since 1986 it has built up information on 15 million investments. De-duplicated, this comes to more than seven million names in over four million investing households.

Financial Times Business Lists offers addresses of purchasers of high-cost management and industry reports; financial book buyers; subscribers to *FT* sister publications, such as *Investors Chronicle*; specialist newsletter subscribers; and purchasers of *FT* diaries. These are live computerized lists which *Financial*

Times Business Information has to update for its own purposes.

Dun and Bradstreet's Dun's Marketing has a 400 000 strong file of actively trading businesses extracted from D&B's overall database of 1.4 million businesses. This supplementary file offers selection by standard industrial classification codes (SIC codes), size of company by turnover or employees, and location at start-up date, and includes one million named executives. Dun and Bradstreet are keen on quality, and have taken the trouble to reduce 'gone-aways' by pruning 150 000 out-of-date records. They guarantee a refund if a mailing using their database has more than 3.5 per cent 'gone-aways'. Their experience points to the danger of a database on which it may be easier to include than exclude an address. How old, how well maintained, is the database you propose using – including your own?

ICS has a list of 380 000 people who have purchased or enquired about self-development and leisure courses. Aged 20–35, approximately 65 per cent male, 35 per cent female.

Catering Digest has a database of 250 000 people concerned with the catering industry, including restaurants, hotels, pubs, canteens, fast food outlets and local authority caterers.

The above is just a sample of ready-made specialist lists on computer which may be useful to you.

TARGETING

Targeting is the name of the game, an answer to junk mail as far as selectivity goes – although what is junk mail can still remain with the recipient's reaction. Targeting is the means of cutting costs and maximizing response. It brings direct mail (and mail drops) in line with traditional above-the-line media planning and buying.

You may or may not agree with this, but it has been proposed that an indication of age group in a list consisting of names and addresses is the give-away first name. These first names tend to belong to particular periods and are associated with factors like the popularity of film stars and pop singers or the occurrence of royal marriages.

In 1987 a survey of 43 million adults identified the ages associated with 13 000 first names. It arrived at the projection that Florence and Percy are retired, Eileen and Dennis have matured families, Pamela and Keith have young families, and Sharon and Kevin are probably still single and without families.

This survey was conducted by CACI, and used the first names of 43 million adults on the ACORN list as compiled by the credit reference agency UAPT INFOLINK. It identified the age profiles by linking the neighbourhoods in which names were located with the age profiles of those neighbourhoods as described in CACI's 1985 small-area population model.

The result was CACI's Monica database. It predicts the likely age group of customers and direct mail prospects on the basis of their first names. CACI believe that 75 per cent of the British adult population have a first name which is a good indicator of age.

Some names have endured longer than others. Paul and Sarah are associated with both groups 1 and 2 (pre-family and young family), while Arthur and Dorothy are found in both groups 3 and 4 (mature family and retired). Names with the weakest age profiles are male names such as Robert and Gordon, and yet a seemingly old favourite like John was particularly popular for babies born in the 1940s and 1950s.

The cost of applying Monica as an overlay to mailings from the ACORN list is £10 per thousand selected names.

The basis of much targeting is geodemographic targeting using the ACORN, PIN or MOSAIC systems. ACORN (a classification of residential neighbourhoods) is operated by CACI Market Analysis; PIN (Pinpoint identified neighbourhoods) is run by Pinpoint Analysis Ltd; and MOSAIC is the system provided by CCN Systems Ltd. The addresses will be found at the end of the book. They are based on census enumeration districts and postcodes, ACORN identifying 38 neighbourhood types, PIN 60, and MOSAIC 58. Yet another system, Super Profiles, developed by McIntyre Marketing, breaks the population down into 150 neighbourhood types.

With these systems, it is possible to locate people according to where they live, and the companies concerned rent lists according to choice of neighbourhood.

Pinpoint found there were discrepancies in the Post Office's central postcode directory and the file of census enumeration districts provided by the Office of Population Censuses and Surveys, and so created its own classifications. Census enumeration districts consist of about 150 households or 400 people, while postcodes each embrace about 15 addresses. The Pinpoint address code (PAC) locates each of the 22 million domestic addresses in Britain within one metre.

There is also a FinPin system which identifies people with the characteristics appropriate to a particular product or service, in particular financial categories. FinPin identifies and locates 40 categories of people, such as married couples in their fifties and early sixties whose children have left home and who have high disposable incomes – the 'wealthy empty nesters'.

The ACORN and MOSAIC profiles shown represent 40 million home addresses, explain their neighbourhood selection processes, and make interesting comparisons. They are adjusted from time to time.

ACORN PROFILE, GREAT BRITAIN

Acorn groups		1981 population	per cent
A	Agricultural areas	1 811 485	3.4
B	Modern family housing, higher incomes	8 667 137	16.2
C	Older housing of intermediate status	9 420 477	17.6
D	Poor quality older terraced housing	2 320 846	4.3
E	Better-off council estates	6 976 570	13.0
F	Less-well-off council estates	5 032 657	9.4
G	Poorest council estates	4 048 658	7.6
H	Multiracial areas	2 086 026	3.9
I	High-status non-family areas	2 248 207	4.2
J	Affluent suburban housing	8 514 878	15.9
K	Better-off retirement areas	2 041 338	3.8
U	Unclassified	388 632	0.7
Acorn types			
A	1 Agricultural villages	1 376 427	2.6
A	3 Areas of farms and smallholdings	435 058	0.8
B	3 Cheap modern private housing	2 209 759	4.1

B	4	Recent private housing, young families	1 648 534	3.1
B	5	Modern private housing, older children	3 121 453	5.8
B	6	New detached houses, young families	1 404 893	2.6
B	7	Military bases	282 498	0.5
C	8	Mixed owner-occupied and council estates	1 880 142	3.5
C	9	Small town centres and flats above shops	2 157 360	4.0
C	10	Villages with non-farm employment	2 463 246	4.6
C	11	Older private housing, skilled workers	2 919 729	5.5
D	12	Unimproved terraces with old people	1 351 877	2.5
D	13	Pre-1914 terraces, low-income families	762 266	1.4
D	14	Tenement flats lacking amenities	206 703	0.4
E	15	Council estates, well-off older workers	1 916 242	3.6
E	16	Recent council estates	1 392 961	2.6
E	17	Council estates, well-off young workers	2 615 376	4.9
E	18	Small council houses, often Scottish	1 051 991	2.0
F	19	Low-rise estates in industrial towns	2 538 119	4.7
F	20	Inter-war council estates, older people	1 667 994	3.1
F	21	Council housing for the elderly	826 544	1.5
G	22	New council estates in inner cities	1 079 351	2.0
G	23	Overspill estates, high unemployment	1 729 757	3.2
G	24	Council estates with overcrowding	868 141	1.6
G	25	Council estates with worst poverty	371 409	0.7
H	26	Multi-occupied terraces, poor Asians	204 493	0.4
H	27	Owner-occupied terraces with Asians	577 871	1.1
H	28	Multilet housing with Afro-Caribbeans	387 169	0.7
H	29	Better off multi-ethnic areas	916 493	1.7
I	30	High-status areas, few children	1 129 079	2.1
I	31	Multilet big old houses and flats	822 017	1.5
I	32	Furnished flats, mostly single people	297 111	0.6
J	33	Inter-war semis, white collar workers	3 054 032	5.7
J	34	Spacious inter-war semis, big gardens	2 676 598	5.0
J	35	Villages with wealthy older commuters	1 533 756	2.9
J	36	Detached houses, exclusive suburbs	1 250 492	2.3
K	37	Private houses, well-off elderly	1 199 703	2.2
K	38	Private flats with single pensioners	841 635	1.6
U	39	Unclassified	388 632	0.7

Area total	53 556 911	100.0

Crown copyright/CACI copyright

MOSAIC TYPES
AND THEIR NATIONAL PENETRATION

Type		*% GB households*
M1	High-status retirement areas with many single pensioners	1.0
M2	High-status retirement areas, married owner-occupiers	0.4
M3	High-status retirement areas with rented flats for elderly	0.2
M4	Boarding houses and lodgings, many in retirement areas	1.9
M5	Inter-war O/O housing, commercial and managerial cadres	4.2
M6	Elite prof/educational suburbs, mostly inner metropolitan	2.1
M7	High-status family enclaves in inner city areas	0.5
M8	Highest income and status areas, mostly outer metropolitan	0.9
M9	Inter-war semis, white collar commuters to urban office jobs	4.7
M10	Inter-war semis, owner-occupied by well-paid manual workers	5.0
m11	Areas of mixed tenure, many old people	3.2
M12	Lower-income enclaves in high-income suburbs	0.1
M13	Older suburbs, young families in gov't and service employment	4.6
M14	Older terraces, owner-occupied by craft manual workers	2.5
M15	Lower-income older terraced housing	1.5
M16	Overcrowded older houses, often in areas of housing shortage	1.8
M17	Older terraces, young families in very crowded conditions	0.5
M18	Tenements, caravans and other rented temporary accommodation	0.2
M19	Town centres and flats above shops	2.9
M20	Rented non-family inner city areas with financial problems	0.7
M21	Low-status inner suburbs with subdivided older housing	1.0
M22	Older housing where owner-occupiers often share with tenants	0.7

M23 Purpose-built private flats, single people in service jobs   2.8
M24 Divided houses with mobile single people and few
    children   0.5
M25 Smart inner city flats, company lets, very few children   1.5
M26 Post-1981 housing in non-family urban and city centres   0.9
M27 Post-1981 housing replacing older terraces   0.7
M28 Newly built council housing, mostly high-density
    inner city   1.4
M29 Newly built inner cities estates with non-family
    populations   1.0
M30 Post-1981 extensions to high-stress inner city estates   0.4
M31 High-unemployment estates with worst financial
    problems   2.4
M32 Council estates with the highest levels of unemployment   0.3
M33 Council estates, often Scottish flats, with worst
    overcrowding   1.3
M34 Better council estates but with financial problems   2.2
M35 Low-rise council housing, low incomes and serious
    deprivation   1.7
M36 Areas with some public housing for elderly   2.7
M37 Council estates, mostly Scottish, middle-income small
    houses   1.9
M38 Council estates in factory towns with settled older
    workers   2.1
M39 Quality 1930s and 1950s overspill estates, now with
    old people   3.0
M40 Best quality council housing in areas of low
    unemployment   5.2
M41 New greenfield council estates with many young
    children   1.8
M42 Post-1981 council housing, higher incomes   0.4
M43 Post-1981 council housing, few families   0.8
M44 Post-1981 council housing with stable families   0.7
M45 Military accommodation   0.4
M46 Post-1981 housing in areas of highest income and status   0.2
M47 Highest income and status areas, newish family housing   1.1
M48 Post-war private estates with children of school age   3.1
M49 Newly built private estates, high-income young families   1.8
M50 Newly built private estates, factory workers, young
    families   3.3
M51 Post-1981 extensions to private estates   1.4

M52 Post-1981 housing in established older suburbs   1.8
M53 New commuter estates in rural areas   2.1
M54 Villages with some non-agricultural employment   3.1
M55 Pretty rural villages with wealthy long–distance
     commuters   3.7
M56 Agricultural villages   2.0
M57 Hamlets and scattered farms   0.7
M58 Unclassified   0.1

The Consumer Location System (CLS) developed by the Royal Mail and available from the Direct Mail Sales Bureau (see Chapter 19) is a computerized method of analysing people's purchasing, reading and viewing habits, and relating them to the neighbourhoods in which they live.

This refined consumer profile relates to propensity to consume. To do this it takes data from research sources such as Target Group Index (TGI), Financial Research Services (FRS) and AGB Home Audit, analyses markets so defined, and couples this with ACORN and other area classifications. Using ACORN and the electoral register it is possible to choose people who are the types identified by the CLS.

This is but a brief sketch of the CLS, and the system is more fully explained in a Royal Mail brochure. The format is explained by the accompanying chart.

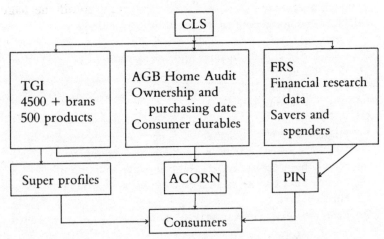

POSTCODES

Royal Mail postcodes are a means of achieving prompt delivery, especially when combined with the optical character recognition system in mechanical letter offices (see Chapter 8). The Postcode Address File (PAF) contains the address and postcode for every address in Britain, more than 23.5 million of them. PAF is available in directories and on microfiche, magnetic tape and disc. On one 4.7 inch compact disc, PAF can help you check addresses in records. It requires a CD-ROM drive to read it, and costs about £3000 plus VAT.

However, there are many PAF facilities available from the Post Office. Whatever way you choose to roll out mailings it is worth remembering that the Post Office offers discounts for fully postcoded mailings. Special PAF services from the Post Office include the supply of paper-based labels in combinations of postcodes as required. Postcode maps are available from Post Office headquarters, and also from John Bartholomew & Son and Geographia Ltd.

You may find PAF useful to identify geographic sales areas; target zones; plan distribution systems; rate different areas; analyse results of campaigns; and cut data access or input costs.

But essentially postcoding aids more efficient handling of mail, and it is therefore advantageous to make sure that all mail is postcoded. This can start by requesting postcodes on coupons and order forms. It applies as much to off-the-page promotions as to direct mail and mailing lists.

PIGGYBACKING

Another option which may be useful to you in both targeting and effecting economy is what is variously known as piggybacking, bounceback, third-party mailing, or swap mailing. Your shot is inserted with someone else's mailing when the list is appropriately targeted. A typical example is the sort of insertion you often find with your monthly or quarterly bill. Or it could be a product despatch insertion put inside a parcel or package.

There are certain merits and demerits in piggybacking.

There is a saving in postage and the recipient has only one envelope to open. If your shot is of interest to the recipient, all well and good, but it can be an irritant if the recipient wants to read the bill and finds extraneous pieces of paper in the envelope. In the case of the parcel, the recipient will probably want to look at the goods and not be deterred by irrelevant insertions. So much depends on the *relevance* of the insertion. If it adds something of interest and value to the original mailing, good. A buyer of records, cassettes or discs may be interested in associated equipment from another supplier.

One wonders about catalogues (which seem to be selling identical merchandise under different suppliers' names). They may not always be appreciated with bills from credit card companies and public utilities.

On the other hand a 'match the shapes' bingo–type scratch card from Kays, with full–colour pictures of gifts, and a reply card on the reverse side, was a neat, amusing and attractive insert with electricity bills.

But what was to be made of this pink panther effort? The pink and grey envelope with jigsaw pattern was from Kaleidoscope, and bore the words 'IMPORTANT – OPEN NOW FOR SOME EXCITING SAVINGS NEWS FROM KALEIDOSCOPE'. Inside was an enigmatic leaflet offering a free Sheaffer ballpen, another leaflet about four free wine glasses or a clock radio, a folder about a Sun Alliance Money Maker insurance scheme, an A4 application form, a letter on Kaleidoscope heading which began 'Dear Mr. . . , As you know Kaleidoscope like to bring you exciting quality goods' which went on to sell the Sun Alliance scheme, and a business reply envelope addressed to Sun Alliance. Throughout, a jigsaw theme was used which was too clever by half. The words 'As you know' are a favourite cliché of sales letter writers, and should be avoided.

But how confusing was this mail shot! What had Sun Alliance got to do with Kaleidoscope? Why couldn't Sun Alliance write direct? Why did it need the recommendation of an utterly irrelevant company? Piggybacking can go too far.

Why pink? Was this perhaps thought attractive to women? The mailing was to both sexes. And for sceptics the word

'IMPORTANT' on the printed envelope was sufficient of a turn-off to get the shot discarded without the recipient bothering to open it. Why do direct marketers give the kiss of death by pronouncing that it *is* probably junk mail?

5   Insertions

What should comprise a complete mail shot?

Other chapters discuss individual items from sales letters to gimmicks, and one chapter is devoted to the one-piece mailer. In this short chapter let us consider what may be included in a mail shot and for what purpose.

If several enclosures are necessary, the order in which they should be taken out of the envelope – even the way up – can be important. This tactic is not always observed, and upon opening the envelope the recipient does not know what to read first. A drill for collation and filing should be planned. This is elementary advice, but why is it so rarely observed?

Here are some pertinent questions for you to ask yourself.

1   Is a sales letter sufficient? Do you really need enclosures?
2   What is the minimum necessary content of your mail shot? An essential combination might be a sales letter, order form and reply envelope.
3   Will the cost of insertions really be justified by either response or *increased* response (note that the two are different)? Are you trying too hard?
4   Will the weight of insertions increase the cost of postage, and is this extra cost likely to be justified by better results?
5   Will insertions increase the envelope size, and will that extra cost be justified by results? As we shall see in Chapter 8, envelope size has a psychological effect on which envelopes to open first.
6   What does the recipient need to find in the envelope in order to be sufficiently interested and convinced to take positive action?
7   Are your proposed insertions likely to be helpful and

action-provoking, or confusing, discouraging and extravagant? To help you to decide, collect the mailings you receive yourself and judge your own reactions. If you want a second or third opinion, ask your spouse or secretary to do the same.

8   Is the bulk of the envelope likely to create a bad impression *before* the envelope is opened? Will you merely tempt people to say 'It's only junk mail'?

9   Do you need a sales letter at all? Is a folder, brochure or catalogue sufficient by itself? Is a one-piece mailer adequate?

The art of good advertising is *simplicity*. Do your insertions comply with this basic rule? Let us consider some of the reasons why simplicity is so important.

Your mailing is probably unsolicited and unexpected. It may benefit from an element of surprise and be welcomed, but this is becoming increasingly unlikely. Mail to commercial addresses can add to the burden of correspondence. A secretary may well segregate obvious direct mail from apparently real business correspondence. She may even open large envelopes last! Mail to domestic addresses may have to compete with other direct mail shots. If it is the only mail received it could be disappointing since it is not personal mail.

When planning a mailing you should try to anticipate the likely reaction when it is received. Sales resistance needs to be minimized. A DL envelope may be better received than something larger. Window envelopes may save double addressing, but they suggest a business rather than a private letter, and probably a bill. Or do you think it is unfair to delude people with a plain DL envelope? Envelopes will be discussed in Chapter 8, but the question does arise here in relation to insertions. These are all for you to worry about, whether you are producing the mail shot or considering a scheme put up by a mailing house.

It is not a matter of being penny-pinching, yet you do need to be mean about your budget from the point of view of cost efficiency, which means getting the most business at the least cost. Designers may well concentrate on being creative rather than on necessity, utility and economy. When giving a brief to a direct mail house or studio you must first determine what *you* want. Costs will be discussed more fully in Chapter 7.

This comes right back to your budget: how much do you plan to pay per shot? It is no different from planning a press or TV budget for so many insertions or appearances, but it can also be dependent on production cost. Very easily, money can vanish on elaborate mailings that may be no more effective than something more simple. Complicated shots can deter response, however ingenious you may think or be told they are.

It is necessary to achieve understanding of your offer *as quickly as possible*. Interest is easily lost or diverted, so it pays to get to the point as soon as you can. Don't frustrate understanding and interest because your mailing is too fussy.

The *sincerity* of your offer can be enhanced by its simplicity of attack. This goodwill element can be overshadowed by elaborate shots. People are not going to sit down and meticulously study every word and every item if you overwhelm them with long letters and too many enclosures.

Response is more easily won if you make it *easy* to decide and act. But if there is temptation to put it aside and deal with it when the recipient has more time, that time may never come. The problem with most printed advertising is that it is static and silent, and somehow you have to prod the recipient into taking action. It is the recipient who is neither static nor silent. How do you exploit this completely opposite ability? A reduction in time between your effort and his or her effort can be the difference between acceptance and refusal. Again, this points to the persuasive power of simplicity.

Another way to promote action is curiosity. Does your mailer have this quality? Too-clever 'teaser' tactics can be irritating, but if you use some device – like posing an unusual question in the first paragraph of the sales letter – you can overcome the static nature of the medium. Put a smirk on the face of the reader, make him raise his eyebrows or nod his head. *Provoke physical response if you can.*

As you will see in the next chapter, the one-piece mailer has the merit of simplicity, and it can create curiosity and move the recipient to take action.

6   One-piece mailers

The contents of mailers and how to keep down costs are discussed in other chapters, but the single-piece complete-in-itself mail shot has very definite advantages. That has been my experience.

It may, of course, be essential to have more than one item. A sales letter may be necessary to introduce a catalogue or to highlight certain new items in it. Much depends on your kind of business, and it would be pedantic to favour only one type of mailer. You must decide what is most likely to work best for you. In my business, I prefer the one-piece mailer. Everything they want to know is there on one piece of paper, from which the order form can be detached. Some people photocopy the order form and retain the mailer intact.

A one-piece mailer says and does everything within one piece of print. The order form can even be detached and folded to form a business reply item, thus saving a reply envelope. The mailer can be a folder or a booklet, but one large sheet of paper folding down like a map has the following special merits.

1   The broadsheet can fold down to a convenient envelope size such as DL or 9×4 in (229×102 mm) pocket. But watch the size of the sheet and the weight of the paper, otherwise it will be difficult to fill envelopes if the mailer is too thick. You may have to use 80 rather than $100g/m^2$ paper, or have six rather than eight panels. If you are mailing overseas, it will be economical to keep the total weight of the mailer and envelope to within 20 g. Tests should be made with sample papers and envelopes before ordering print.

2   The whole shot is compact and attractive to the recipient. Everything he wants to know is there whenever he wants it. This may be there and then – or when he refers to it again. He can even put it in his inside pocket. The convenience factor is very strong.

3   It encourages immediate attention because of the size of envelope. There is a curious psychology about envelopes which is worth repeating here. If you open your own post, which envelopes do you select first? Most people open the smaller business size envelopes first because they expect them to be the most important. They may perhaps contain cheques! Window envelopes, especially the smaller ones, usually contain bills. Large envelopes are less likely to contain business letters and are often left to last. The one-piece mailer in a DL or 9 × 4 in envelope asks to be opened along with the most important mail.

4   Because it has folds, and if the front pane or panel is intriguing, curiosity encourages your prospect to unfold the mailer to see what's inside. If you can induce curiosity you have captured the reader's attention. And if your sequence of information is well arranged the concertina effect – like some of those amusing birthday cards – will lead the recipient on and on through your sales message. You have created *action* on the part of the reader! He or she is automatically impelled to absorb what you have to say. In the end, the reader can have a complete spread of information which is not confined to separate panels but, like a map, is landscape in presentation. Your apparently small mail shot becomes impressively big.

5   It is easy to fill in the envelope, but insert it so that when it is taken out the top front is visible first.

POINTS TO CONSIDER

There are a few special points to remember about one-piece mailers:

1   The whole sheet should be designed so that the folds – and the unfolding – do follow a coherent sequence. It

shouldn't be necessary to have to turn the sheet upside down. This applies to the layout of both sides.

2 The front panel – the part that is immediately visible – should not just be a title but should be either a digest of the contents or, in some way, a means of attracting attention and urging the recipient to unfold the mailer. One device is to use a cut-out to reveal part of a picture inside.

3 The address and telephone number should be clearly displayed and easily found, and repeated if necessary. Don't make the mistake of putting it on the order form only. If this is detached and mailed the customer is left with no identity or location if this is needed later on.

4 The order form should be positioned where it is easiest to cut out – for instance, in a position with two outside edges. It may help to print a dotted line round the two inside edges of the order form. Otherwise people may be inclined to return the whole mailer, which can be a nuisance to you.

5 In every way, when planning the layout of the mailer think how it can be most convenient, to both the recipient and to you. Similarly, make it easy for the customer to find out what he needs to know, and easy for him to order what he wants. For instance, if there are several items on the order form provide a small box against each item (and maybe price) which can be ticked to show exactly which item or choice is required.

If there is a choice of colours of, say, a garment it is a good idea to ask for second choice. If you are out of stock of one colour, the second choice will avoid unnecessary apologetic correspondence. Prices should state whether they are inclusive of postage, or whether postage has to be added, and the same applies to VAT. Don't assume that the customer will know that postage or VAT are included in your price.

It may be a psychological mistake to make a price look cheaper because these items have not been included, and people may resent the hidden extras. If your mailing is to both home and overseas prospects, make sure you have separate prices such as airmail prices. Postage abroad can be many times greater than internal post.

Again, with overseas mailings insist on cash with order, and preferably in sterling to avoid currency charges. Unless you have some special agency arrangement, never give credit to anyone overseas, for you have no means of recovering foreign debts. Our banks have discovered that!

What the customer needs to know is important. It is easy for you to know what you know, but is the given information so explicit that the reader cannot be puzzled or annoyed and cannot make a mistake? An uncertain customer is a lost one.

In most cases the prospect will not take the trouble to write or phone to ask what you haven't told him. It is up to you to think of every possible reason why your prospect may hesitate to order, and have an answer to his doubt. Have you left anything out?

What must you tell him to convince him and so secure his order? Does he need to know how long it will take to deliver the goods? Is there immediate delivery on receipt of cheque? Or do you wait for a cheque to be accepted by the bank? Must the order be prepaid, or will you invoice? 'Send no money now' may be a good inducement, or it could create bad debts! To whom should cheques be made payable? Do you advise registered post for payments, especially from overseas? Do you accept only sterling from abroad? Do you accept credit cards? Is it a dated offer? Do you supply on approval? What a lot of questions – but getting paid or making it easy to pay *are* important, whichever way round you look at it.

All such details should be made clear, 'absolutely clear' as the politicians say. You do not want to get involved in time-wasting correspondence or telephone calls. Nor do you want to get bogged down in debt collecting. People who owe you money generally get to hate you. You must not deter orders simply because you have failed to put yourself in your prospect's shoes. He is not an idiot: *but he simply does not know unless you tell him.*

And while the wording needs to be fully detailed and free of ambiguity, it should be given briefly. Use short words, short sentences, short paragraphs. Set it out well with subheadings and good use of white space so that there is not a formidable amount of grey reading matter. Introduce contrast such as subheadings in a bold or different typeface. Don't frighten people off by making the mailer look a boring mass of words.

People do want to know everything that will interest them and give them confidence in making a purchase, but people tend not to read and they can be quite lazy about reading. Perhaps this is a result of television? There is therefore a contradiction here which has to be resolved. A lot of words may be necessary, but you must not make them look a lot!

If they don't want to read, how do you overcome this problem? Photographs, sketches, cartoons and diagrams can help. It is true that a picture can tell more than a thousand words, as any horticultural catalogue will demonstrate. It is no use saying a pansy is a pretty flower unless people can see its face and colours. There are people who don't know what a pansy looks like or, if they do, what it is called. *Remember this when describing goods.* Sometimes there are trade names and popular names. Think how many flowers are just called 'daisies' – and you want to call them gerberas or asters!

Even a picture of a person, real or otherwise, can communicate a message more effectively or convincingly than mere words. This may be a picture of you, or of a model using your product, or a drawing of a typical user. You don't have to use something ridiculous like a bikini-clad blonde wearing high-heel shoes and driving a power mower (it's been done), but people often identify themselves with pictures. A woman may buy a dress because a pretty girl is wearing it. She wants to look like that pretty girl. Maybe she thinks she still is a pretty girl.

A very simple way of emphasizing or pinpointing items is to use a second colour for subheadings, or to set black type on a coloured panel. But don't use too hard a background colour which kills the wording. Also, be careful of reversing type to read white on a colour. Unless the wording is very large to effect good contrast, 50 per cent of the legibility can be lost by reversing small type.

You may not be a designer or a copywriter, and you may have to rely on outsiders for creativity, but only you can put yourself in the place of your customer. It is therefore an important task to be a good communicator. You need to ask yourself: what does your prospect need to know, what do you need to tell him, and what do you need to know from him, if business is to result from your mailer?

In this way you can both brief the designer or writer clearly and fully, and criticize creative work. Then you will get what you want. Beware of clever designers who cannot communicate. They may be concerned with the eye, but you are concerned with the mind.

7   How to control costs

The cost of direct marketing will figure in your overall budget of costs, plus profit margin, by which you arrive at price. Advertising is a distribution cost which has to be recovered by price. Ultimately it is paid for by your customer or client – unless you fail to achieve profitable sales.

Promotional costs are part of price. Remember that. They do *not* come out of profits. They are not 'what you can afford' other than as a legitimate investment in making a profit. They have to be seen alongside all other costs such as the purchase of goods for resale, office administration, packing, salaries, overheads and so on. Promotion is just *one* item in the total budget.

The question is how to *control* costs, that is how to gain the greatest reward from the least expenditure. Here are some essential areas to consider:

Postage   This is a major cost, and there are several ways by which it can be controlled, minimized or even reduced.
Number of items   What is the minimum necessary number?
Weight of items
Print costs   Sound print buying is a key to costs.
Quantity of mailing   Selective use of mailing lists, and how they are obtained and maintained.
Media buying   This applies where media other than direct mail and mail drops are used. It involves use of media research data.

Of these, postage, numbers and print costs are related. Let us consider how economies can be effected in these six areas.

Postage
There are two ways of controlling postage costs: by keeping down the weight, and by taking advantage of Post Office rebates.

Reference was made in the previous chapter to quantity discounts on business reply or Freepost items. There are also rebates if you send more than 4250 identical presorted letters or packets, discounts being on a sliding scale according to quantity; however, delivery is normally only within seven days after posting. For speedier deliveries there is the second-class discount service, on a contract basis, for mail presorted into post towns (12 per cent discount) or countries (7 per cent discount). There is a similar first-class letter contracts service for a minimum of 5000 same size and weight details, sorted to post towns, to earn a 13 per cent discount. The full details are given in a Royal Mail booklet *Letter Discount Services for the Businessman* available from the Post Office Direct Mail Section, Room 195, 33 Grosvenor Place, London SW1X 1EE.

Post Office and other bulk services for overseas mail will be discussed in Chapter 18.

However, be warned! David Brech, marketing manager of Royal Mail Letters, said on October 15, 1987 (*Marketing* report): 'We are determined to protect the consumer's interests. . . . We need to do away with the junk mail image.' The Post Office threatened to withdraw rebate schemes from mail users who failed to meet its quality standards. At the time of writing, the Post Office was experimenting with a mail sort scheme to replace the rebate schemes mentioned above.

Number of items
Exactly how many items are essential? Each item represents a printing cost, and can increase the weight and therefore the postage cost. Can you keep within the basic 60 g? Weighty items like catalogues may well take you into the 100 g rate, which is quite a jump in postage cost, even with a rebate.

Weight of items
What will be the weight of print items? Before ordering print it is sensible to ask the printer for paper samples, and to weigh

dummies made up to the sheet size or number of pages of your intended items. Paper can be surprisingly heavy. By experimenting with paper samples you can decide whether to use, say, 80, 90 or 100g/m² paper. And don't forget to include the weight of the envelope.

The paper size, or number of pages of a catalogue, may have to be considered from the point of view of weight. This can be a critical consideration with overseas mailings. As with newspapers, you may find it necessary to use different weights of paper for UK and overseas mailings; the basic weight for overseas mail is 20 g not 60 g.

Print costs

Nowadays, modern offset litho printing can offer full-colour work at reasonable cost, but quotations should be invited from more than one printer. Their prices for the same job can vary considerably, often due to their use of different machines. Moreover, some printers are more helpful than others in their advice on paper, typography and design. If you visit printers and check out what equipment and services they have, this will be beneficial. Printers are craftsmen, proud of the skills which you can enjoy. More about this in Chapter 11.

Quantity of mailing

What is the most economical volume for your mailing? This will depend on a combination of mailing list size, cost of postage and envelopes, and printing costs. The run-on cost for extra leaflets may look attractively economical, but you still have all the other costs to bear. Quantity will also be related to the sales target. What is the minimum mailing that is likely to achieve the sales target and avoid wastage? When you see some of the blanket mailings put out by some direct marketers it would seem that costing is ignored, and that the selectivity of direct mail has been forgotten.

Media buying

When above-the-line media such as press and television are used, it is probable that a direct marketing advertising agency will be necessary, as in the cases of large off-the-page direct response marketers. Media planning is based on the use of ABC circulation figures, JICNARS readership figures and BARB television audience figures. Circulation means audited average net sales over a period, usually six months. Readership means the estimated number of readers, plus their demographic details, based on social grades representing occupation, and is obtained by marketing research surveys. BARB uses a sample of viewers to produce audience figures for both BBC and ITV programmes.

These statistics can help you or your agency to prepare media schedules so that your advertisement will be addressed to your target audience as economically as possible. Media choices will be based on cost-per-thousand circulation or readership, demographic characteristics and elimination of duplication.

Thus an agency will be used as much for media planning and buying skills as for creativity. In fact, there are today not only agencies which specialize in direct response marketing, but media independents and creative à la carte agencies.

But you may not be big enough to need an agency, and you will handle your own media buying. If so, you should study very carefully the relative abilities of different publications to reach your market – and to do so as economically as possible. Your choice may be based on past experience, and methods of researching results will be discussed in Chapter 16.

GETTING THE BEST FROM YOUR MEDIA BUDGET

An excellent idea of what can be involved in careful budgeting was set out in an advertisement from Direct Response Media, Westminster House, Kew Road, Richmond, Surrey TW9 2ND which appeared in *Direct Response*, from which the following is quoted:

Fifteen important media questions vital to direct marketers
1 Do you like the idea of paying 5 per cent media commission (or even less) instead of the usual 15 per cent?

2 Have you established the best size and page position for your advertisements?

3 Do you know the optimum frequency for each publication?

4 Would you like to extend your peak selling seasons?

5 Do you usually pay extra for premium positions?

6 Are you paying the lowest rate for your space?

7 Have you negotiated CPI deals?

8 What can you learn from your competitors' media schedule?

9 Are you taking full advantage of short-term opportunities?

10 How quickly can you weed out non-effective media?

11 What are you learning from A/B tests, regional tests, crossover tests, destruction tests?

12 Are you using the savings from short-term buying to test new media?

13 Are you aware of the new opportunities offered by inserts?

14 Have you seen how effectively television can be used in the direct marketing media mix?

15 Do you want media advice based upon unequalled experience of analysing consumer response?

This advertisement indicates some of the intricacies involved in budgeting direct response marketing which relies on press or television advertising, and points to the advantages of using a specialist agency.

8   Envelopes

The envelope is the package, and like the package for a product it can serve four purposes:

1   It can be printed to identify the sender.
2   It can contain the mail shot.
3   It can protect the contents.
4   It can ensure delivery.

But does the similarity to a product package stop there? Should it be a sort of general package, mute and anonymous, or should it identify and announce the sender?

There are not only contradictory schools of thought here, but also questions of policy and psychology and the tactics of persuasion and promotion.

Whatever you may think about junk mail, most people whether in a private or business capacity are curious about the post. Not only that, but they *expect* the post and are vociferous about delays and late deliveries. Postal services have deteriorated from the days when a letter posted at 9 a.m. was delivered by 6 p.m. the same day, and there were Sunday collections.

Generally, people hope for something good to arrive in the post. Few people are more popular than the postman. Maybe a jolly, colourful envelope adds to the pleasure of receiving the mail. Or is that always the case: has one's welcome been undermined?

The psychology is very different from that regarding any other form of advertising, except perhaps posters which were once called 'the poor man's art gallery'. Mail can be very personal, so let's consider your own attitude. *What do you do when confronted by unopened mail?* It could be a good test to apply to the direct mail you intend sending out.

It is unlikely that your first move will be to slit open the envelope. The first thing most recipients want to know is not so much what is inside but who sent it. They go through the newly arrived post, even study postmarks in the attempt to identify senders. They look at stamps, frankings and printed information on the front of envelopes or on the flaps. Then they decide which ones to open first.

They may be influenced by the styling of their address, whether or not an address label has been used, or by the shape, size or bulk of the envelope. They can be adept at detecting unwanted junk mail, or they will spot mail they have been expecting. This behaviour is particularly true of domestic mail. Your envelope may have to survive this sort of scrutiny if it is to survive, if it is even to succeed in being opened!

The appearance of the envelope can take three forms:

1   It can be an unobtrusive plain envelope.
2   It can have a simple identification, or a return-to-sender address.
3   It can be designed as part of the total mail shot, and you can start selling off the envelope.

Let us consider the three different appearances.

PLAIN ENVELOPES

A simple buff manila envelope, a white or cream laid or woven envelope, or a quality envelope like the Character series from Spicers, may suit your mailing, either because it is economical or you do not want or need to announce your identity with a printed envelope. A quality envelope gives the impression that the contents are important, that the sender is important, or that the recipient is respected.

There are therefore different reasons for using a plain envelope:

1   You need to make your mailing look like normal business correspondence.
2   You need to retain an element of surprise or curiosity, and do not wish to lose this advantage before the envelope is opened.

3   The cost of a printed envelope is not justified; this is a simple budgetary consideration.

4   The final recipient may never see the printed envelope, as with business mail, because the envelope will be opened and discarded by someone else. Printed business envelopes may only please the vanity of the sender, and can be a waste of money.

ENVELOPES WITH PRINTED NAME

The typical printed business envelope exudes pride and looks efficient. It is valuable in business correspondence as distinct from direct response marketing, and quickly identifies mail which may be expected or welcomed such as replies, orders or payments.

A different situation arises with unsolicited direct mail which is unexpected and not necessarily welcomed. The printed business envelope in these circumstances can be a give-away and a turn-off, destroying the element of surprise, and inviting dismissal without even being opened. You need to be careful about provoking a negative reaction. What reaction can you reasonably expect? Have you already established a welcome? Perhaps your brochure *is* expected.

SPECIALLY DESIGNED ENVELOPES

Two things are possible with specially designed envelopes, using colour, pictures or a printed message:

1   You can start selling off the envelope.
2   You can destroy all interest in the envelope's content.

Reader's Digest mailings are sometimes criticized, but this has not stopped *Reader's Digest* from using its hard-selling tactics; so they must work. What happens? Some people throw them away unopened, but other people who have previously bought *Reader's Digest* books, records or cassettes open them because they are satisfied customers. Others may be tempted by the prize offers which, after all, appeal to that primary instinct of greed.

It is easiest to sell off the envelope when:

1 The item has been requested, as when a coupon in a press advertisement has been sent in. You can exploit the anticipation.
2 The recipient is a regular customer who is interested in your latest offer.
3 There is something novel about the offer, and the envelope can arouse instant attention, interest, curiosity and anticipation. Prizes are sometimes announced on the envelope.

This is an aspect of direct response marketing where the envelope printers offer a great array of ingenuity with designs, shapes and special types of envelope. A selection of suppliers is given at the end of the book.

SPECIAL TYPES OR USES OF ENVELOPES

Reply envelopes

A reply envelope may seem to be an elementary component, but can it contribute to response and be more than a courtesy?

You may think it sufficient to have an envelope bearing your postal address. You will no doubt make sure that it fits into the outer envelope without folding. It may have to be a shape and size which accepts the order form or payment card without folding it, perhaps for computer handling reasons.

One way to encourage return is to make it a business reply or Freepost envelope. People do not always have stamps. They may want to reply at the weekend. The convenience of a reply-paid envelope can induce return-of-post replies. Post Office services are described later in this chapter.

To avoid problems at your end it may be sensible to print reminders under the flap: 'Have you included your cheque?' or 'Have you put your full postal address on your order?' The latter may seem a needless injunction, but people do write 'M/C' for Manchester. Others may be unaware that many town names are repeated throughout the country: which Sutton, Newport, Dudley or Newcastle is it? Headaches can be prevented by printing reminders on your reply envelope. If coupons or order forms specify county and postcode (and country for overseas orders), time, misdirected orders and complaints can be avoided.

Envelopes can also carry the order form on the reverse side. This saves an extra print item, and helps to simplify response. A typical example is that used by film processing companies. Very explicit instructions are printed on these envelopes. They can be one-piece mailers, serving also as magazine inserts and door-to-door mail drops.

INSERT ENVELOPES

Some mailings include other envelopes which contain special inducements or prize offers. Be careful not to overload a mail shot, but if such an item will attract extra attention, provoke curiosity and increase the response rate, then use it. But some insert envelopes complicate mailings, are out of character with the rest of the shot and may even annoy recipients.

So many people do use sealed insert envelopes, either plain or printed, but you should consider very carefully whether it will really work in your case, or only add to the cost. Copycat mailings are not always wise. It may be that insert envelopes help to overcome the static nature of print by making the recipient do something. Much depends on the wording printed on the envelope, and whether the contents produce a good reaction when extracted.

TEAR-OFF FLAP ENVELOPES

Another device – which can be helpful to the recipient and again give the recipient a participatory role – is the envelope with a perforated deep flap or stub, or bangtail. Usually it is an order form, but it can serve special purposes such as requesting information about other products or services, prize entry forms, or giving the names and addresses of friends. The latter can also offer gifts for enrolling friends. A variety of such envelopes are made by Tompla UK, the international envelope manufacturers who operate in ten European countries.

TRANSPARENT AND SHRINKWRAPPING ENVELOPES

Printed or plain, see-through polythene envelopes are a clean, strong and attractive way of packing large items such as catalogues. Readers will be familiar with them if they receive magazines by mail. A colourful cover will be visible through the polythene, attracting attention more quickly than when, say, a large buff manila or white envelope is used.

There are three special types of polythene envelopes prepared for easy filling, as supplied by firms such as Polymail Plastics Ltd of Westerham, Kent:

Block-headed envelopes are heat sealable and are supplied in blocks of 100 envelopes. The block has two holes so that the filler can attach it to a worktop with screws or dowels. The envelope has a lip with a perforated line. The filler pushes the catalogue into the envelope, and when it is loaded a slight tug is given to free the envelope from the block. This allows speedy wrapping as the envelopes are not loose, and they are half the price of self-seal envelopes. A heat sealer costs £75 and can be supplied with the envelopes.

Wicketed envelopes are similar, are used on semi-automatic machinery, are bunched in 100s and 250s, and have a metal U bracket for easy tear-off. They are used on wrapping machines such as the Norpak and the Sitma.

Self-seal polythene envelopes are more suitable when out-workers are used for filling by hand.

POST OFFICE ENVELOPES AND FACILITIES

When planning a direct mail campaign it is well worth obtaining details of the many Post Office services from Royal Mail Letters, Post Office Direct Mail Section, Room 195, 33 Grosvenor Place, London SW1X 1EE. Some of these services are summarized here.

Freepost
Freepost can be included in your address by your customers

when using their own stationery (second-class service only), or can be printed on your own first- or second-class reply envelopes. In addition to the postage rate on each item, you have to pay an annual licence fee of £20 plus 0.5p handling fee per item received, or 1p per item for first delivery of the day. There are discounts for bulk items of 50 000 or more a year.

Business reply

Envelopes may be printed with the familiar vertical lines, '1' or '2', and the licence number, showing that no stamp is required on a reply envelope. There is a £20 annual licence fee and postage plus handling fee as with Freepost. However, the business reply service is limited to printed envelopes, whereas Freepost can be used generally in your address wherever you may print it, such as in press advertisements and on coupons which require the respondent to address an envelope, as well as on your own printed reply envelopes.

Printed postage impressions

Known as PPIs, these are a preprinted alternative to stamping or franking, and provide ready-stamped envelopes or labels which can be used at any time for minimum numbers of items (for example 5000 letters). They can be used for internal or overseas mail. They cannot be used for reply labels or envelopes. Both printed and computer-generated designs are available. Service indicators are used in the design: 1 for internal first-class letters and certain other mail; 2 for second-class and overseas printed papers; and R for inland rebate services. In addition the words 'postage paid' and the PHQ or office of posting number are shown. There are seven standard designs with notes for printers or studios.

On authorization by the Post Office you are given a serial number and the PHQ or office of posting number. Then you can go ahead and print your own prestamped envelopes, mailing payment for each quantity posted, either in cash or billed through your account.

The service is explained, and specimen designs are contained, in the booklet *Printed Postage Impressions* available from the Royal Mail address given at the beginning of this section.

Postage paid symbol

While printed postage impressions are rather formal, and their convenience may be offset by their 'commercial' appearance, postage paid symbols (PPSs) are the next best thing to a stick-on stamp, and can make an envelope look attractive. The words 'Post 1 Paid' or 'Post 2 Paid' are accompanied by an octagonal PPS bearing the Queen's head in white silhouette on a black or coloured background. Any colour may be used as long as it contrasts with the colour of the envelope. It saves stamp licking or franking and can be applied to any size of envelope.

The colour option can allow you to use your house style and so emphasize your corporate identity. Unlike PPIs (see above) you are not restricted to minimum mailings from a pre-agreed point, and PPSs can be posted anywhere in mainland UK. A minimum quantity of 100 000 must be ordered from the Post Office, and additional wording and illustrations can be printed at the same time if artwork is supplied.

FIRST-DAY COVERS

First-day covers (FDCs) are a kind of free gift. They can have a hit-or-miss effect since not everyone collects stamps or FDCs, but they may be appreciated as souvenirs. Charities sometimes use FDCs on a give-a-gift-get-a-donation basis. This is probably more acceptable and less offensive 'blackmail' than enclosing a coin to be returned with interest, or free Christmas labels which can be a nuisance.

The Post Office, through the British Philatelic Bureau, 20 Brandon Street, Edinburgh EH3 5TT, offers a first-day cover service, using either the Post Office's own printed cover or one of your own design. Foreign FDCs can also be arranged through stamp dealers, and special envelopes are printed by firms which specialize in designing covers.

Optical character recognition

Claimed by the Post Office to be 'the biggest breakthrough in the postal system since the Penny Black', OCR uses a computer in a mechanized letter office (MLO) to machine read envelope addresses and automatically code them, applying phosphor code bars on the envelope. The mail is speeded up since 1000 letters can be coded in two minutes. However, to be effective, mail has to be addressed in an acceptable way.

Envelopes should conform to Post Office preferred (POP) sizes, which are minimum 90 × 140 mm (3½ × 5½ in) up to maximum 120 × 235 mm (4¾ × 9¼ in). Obviously, many of the larger sizes used for direct mail will not conform. The shape of envelope should be rectangular, with the longest edge 1.4 times the shorter edge. They should be made of material weighing at least $63g/m^2$, and postcards should be made from card weighing at least $190g/m^2$.

Addresses should be left-hand adjusted, without punctuation, and the town, county and postcode should be typed in three separate lines. For example:

Mr A. Sample
288 Harrogate Road
BRADFORD
West Yorkshire
BD2 3SP

Fuller details are contained in the OCR booklet available from Royal Mail Letters, 33 Grosvenor Place, London SW1X 1PX.

Your envelope can be your ambassador, your standard bearer or your air raid siren. The choice is yours – but what a splendid choice is provided by envelope makers, envelope printers and the Post Office.

9   Contents of a mail shot

Inevitably some contents of mail shots have come under discussion already. However, here let us consider each possible item, its variations and its special values. Among the additional items which will be featured in this chapter will be novelties and gimmicks.

The contents of a mail shot may therefore consist of combinations of the following:

1 Sales letter.
2 Price list.
3 Order form.
4 Reply envelope.
5 Insert envelope.
6 Money-off voucher.
7 Catalogue.
8 Leaflet, folder or broadsheet.
9 Sample.
10 Novelty or gimmick.

Sales letter
This has been fully discussed in Chapter 3. The question now is whether or not to *have* a sales letter. A one-piece mailer replaces the sales letter. Catalogues sometimes contain a printed letter, but this rather lacks credibility and is impersonal.

A sales letter works best when it does one of two things: contains the proposition, or introduces an enclosure. But it fails if it is too long, tedious and pretentious, as so many are. Unfortunately, sales letters have become to direct response marketing what news releases have to public relations – *bad*!

Yet this can be the most powerful element in a direct mail shot.

Price list

Some mailings consist of this alone, or they may contain an order form and be accompanied by a reply envelope. Many companies as diverse as stationers, stamp dealers, office equipment suppliers, auctioneers, horticultural suppliers and booksellers circulate a price list as distinct from an illustrated catalogue. But it may also be included with other contents of a mail shot. A sales letter may direct attention to new lines or special offers. A price list may be a single sheet of paper, a folder or a wire-stitched booklet.

Order form

An order, enrolment or proposal form may be a separate sheet, a page in a price list or catalogue, a panel in a one-piece mailer, or a deep detachable flap on the reply envelope. From these options you will see that it can be a loose extra item – which may be mislaid – or it can be incorporated in another item. You must decide which is most convenient to both you and your customer, which method helps your budget, and which can contribute to achieving response.

There are several important considerations here which concern the planning of the mail shot. It may be a good idea to design it in such a way that the customer can retain a copy of the order. It forms part of a contract, and there may be legal requirements such as a place to state the age of the respondent. It should be foolproof in making the customer responsible for making a clear order which can be executed correctly so that no query or dispute can arise.

An order form calls for copywriting skills just as much as the sales letter or sales literature. What exactly does the customer want? What exactly do you need? Both require-ments have to be satisfied.

Ambiguity is very easy to achieve. I made the mistake of offering a choice of three items from four, with the word 'or' between the last two choices. To fictionalize this, the choice could have been 'blue, red, green or white'. A number of people sent in money without making a choice – because they had missed the word 'or' – and had to be asked which three they wanted. The choice could not be made for them. This is where it is good practice to provide boxes which can be ticked to indicate choice. People are very careless about filling in forms, but it may be your fault if you do not provide a guiding hand. Never take anything for granted! Always make it simple for people to follow.

Reply envelope

This is both a courtesy and a means of creating action. But it also makes sure that people reply to the right address. Reply envelopes are discussed in Chapter 8.

Insert envelope

This is also discussed in Chapter 8. Do they add extra interest or novelty, excite curiosity, place emphasis on some aspect of the mailing, or give the recipient something to do? Or are they a nuisance; can the reaction on opening the extra envelope be an anticlimax? You can extend your welcome or ruin it.

Some insert envelopes are banal, and underestimate the intelligence of recipients. But if a financial firm is sending out an annual report, statement of account or dividend/interest warrant, it may be propitious to accompany this with a new offer contained in a sealed envelope. This implies that it is important and separate from the main object of the mailing. Moreover, it is contained with something expected or received regularly. It can even be a better way of piggybacking on a regular mailing such as a quarterly gas, electricity or telephone account, although in such cases the envelope must be a small one.

Money-off voucher

A discount voucher may be a means of getting quick response. It may be so much off the price if the goods are ordered by a certain date, and the discount is claimed by means of the voucher. Unit trusts and insurance bonds have been promoted with a set of vouchers so that varying discounts are earned by paying on a succession of dates. Vouchers can also be used if there is a cash payment and credit is not required such as with invoicing. These are referred to again under gimmicks below.

Under this heading can also be included premiums and incentives to buy, submit a larger order, enrol a friend or supply addresses. Some of these incentives can be:

(i) *Speed premiums* when a closing date is given for the offer.

(ii) *Order increase incentive* when gifts, discounts or free postage are offered to orders over a certain volume or price.

(iii) *Sales leads* when a gift is offered if a coupon is returned (such as off-the-page) or further information, catalogues or quotations are requested.

(iv) *Loss leaders* when items, especially in catalogues, are offered at reduced prices (probably at cost) to encourage purchase of regular priced items.

(v) *Mystery gifts* offered for prompt orders – but these should not be so trivial that they invite derision.

(vi) *Gifts for recommendations* when customers are invited to enrol members or supply names of possible customers.

(vii) *Two-step gift leads* when a gift is offered if one offer is accepted, but a better gift is offered if a second more expensive offer is accepted.

(viii) *Continuity incentives* like those of Britannia Music, who offer a second product at a bonus price, and a free one if a certain number of purchases are made.

Catalogue

This may be the sole item, perhaps using a transparent envelope, or there could be an introductory sales letter and other items such as a reply envelope. How far can the catalogue itself serve as virtually a one-piece mailer complete with order form? The order form can be folded and tucked in with a business reply or Freepost envelope.

Leaflet, folder or broadsheet

Sales literature may accompany a sales letter, especially when it is to illustrate the offer or offers, or to give more detailed information. But it is best not to clutter the shot with too many pieces of print. A broadsheet which folds out to form a large display sheet can be a dramatic way of presenting a variety of items, forming a simple catalogue in effect.

Sample

Some products lend themselves to samples if they are flat and do not bulk the envelope. Colour swatches, sachets or specimens can give the recipient a realistic idea of the real thing. This device has been used by fashion houses, coffee manufacturers and paper makers. Publishers send specimen copies or dummies of publications when selling space. Miniature publications have been used effectively to sell both advertisement space and reader subscriptions.

Novelty or gimmick

Now we come to an item where ingenuity can be used to attract attention and give the recipient something to do.

A device once used to promote advertisement space in *Radio Times* was an enclosure which looked like a large ice-cream wafer. On it was printed an instruction to place it in water and see how it expanded as an advertiser's sales would if he advertised in *Radio Times*! The wafer expanded into a Spontex sponge, useful for cleaning the car.

Scratch cards are popular gimmicks, and they often resemble bingo or fruit machines. Kays have used a 'match the shapes' scratch card which illustrates eight free gifts, the reverse side being a reply card, and this was piggybacked on electricity bills. Damart have used a fruit machine style scratch card, again with a reply card on the reverse side.

Dobson and Crowther, the promotional print and packaging firm of Llangollen, have produced some very clever pull-out pockets which reveal cash vouchers and other tokens. Damart have used them. Others are in the form of birthday cards with tabs which reveal discounts when pulled; sealed cards which reveal matching pieces when three sides are torn off; cards with tear-off pictures to reveal gifts; and other impactive mail insertions.

HunterPrint of Corby also design and print imaginative gimmicks such as special envelopes, folders and sealed items, often benefiting from unusual folds. They include coin-rub games and competitions which attract compulsive customer participation. For perfume and cosmetic promotions they can apply fragrances. This is done with a specially formulated solution containing micro-encapsulated particles of perfume which can be applied to the printed material. When the area is rubbed, the fragrance is released!

The gimmick may be in a special form of envelope, one-piece mailer, or sealed item. Specialists in this area are Norman and Burgess of Liverpool, who have produced specially designed pieces which, again, provoke customer participation. The merit of these devices is that they go beyond the formal sales letter, and the sender gains reflected credit for being different.

Pop-ups and cut-outs can also be amusing, lively and memorable. Some of these convert into usable items like pen and pencil holders which can stand on the desk as a permanent reminder. Waterlows of London produce such items as well as scratch-'n'-sniff and coin-reactive ink effects.

Another device is to encapsulate a flat item in a section of transparent plastic to provide a souvenir or even a coaster.

Imaginative ideas like these may enliven a mail shot. Special enclosures are splendid when they do add zest to a mailing, and create an atmosphere of curiosity and excitement and provide a buying incentive.

But these novelties or gimmicks need to be used with care. Don't be stampeded into something which only cheapens your image or credibility. Used unwisely, they can annoy, create suspicion and be too high pressured, and so have a boomerang effect which can destroy an otherwise good offer. If such extra effort is needed to clinch a sale, it may make recipients wonder whether it is such a good offer after all. Why do they have to sell so hard?

A reputable company, or one whose products are known to be excellent (such as those of *Reader's Digest*), may simply set up unnecessary sales resistance. Financial institutions should be reputable, but why *do* so many of them offer free gifts and give themselves a mediocre medicine show image? Many people must realize that nothing is free in this world, and that if they make a purchase the price must include the cost of the gift; or are they such naive and gullible suckers that they cannot resist 'something for nothing'? When they are invited to 'save' it actually means they have to *spend*!

So think about this carefully. A supermarket sells differently from a Bond Street fashion house. It is important to understand the psychology of direct response marketing. You may need to beat the drum or be more discreet. It does not always pay to copy other people. Gimmicks are usually used by people who wish to sell quickly in big quantities to a large market. Even so, do motorists really need a digital alarm clock or a plastic shopping bag when they buy an AA road atlas?

To summarize these remarks, here is a checklist of advantages and disadvantages concerning gimmicks.

Advantages of gimmicks
1   They are creative and enliven a mailing.
2   They overcome the static nature of the medium and induce active participation.
3   They arouse curiosity and, if a prize or discount is involved, they appeal to the acquisitive instinct and human greed.
4   They add to the interest of the mailing, attracting attention to the offer.
5   They can (such as by incentives) produce larger orders.
6   They can be especially effective if you are one of several traders selling similar lines (for example garden seeds) and you want to stand out from the crowd.

Disadvantages of gimmicks
1   They are extra cost items, either reducing profit or increasing price. They have to be paid for one way or another, so there is a budgetary consideration.
2   They may irritate and produce overkill.
3   They may seem unnecessary if the offer is a good one and should be capable of selling on its merits or the reputation of the mailer.
4   They may obscure the offer and be a disincentive.
5   Unless original, they can be regarded as copycat ideas and suffer from dislike of other people's gimmicks.

Quite a lot of points to think about. Perhaps the best time to consider gimmicks is when all else has failed. However, you may think this is contradicted by the fact that some of our biggest and most successful direct marketers use gimmicks all the time. It depends on what sort of mackerel you are.

10   Catalogues

The catalogue is the epitome of armchair selling. Its history reaches back to the Chicago mail order traders Montgomery Ward and Sears Roebuck, who supplied the Midwestern farmers more than a century ago.

Today, catalogues the size of telephone directories can be held on video disc. If the video disc ever replaces the video cassette we may yet see Littlewoods-style catalogues produced for a fraction of the cost and capable of being viewed on TV sets. However, the current tendency is for the big mail order catalogue houses to move towards smaller, more specialized catalogues. A Littlewoods ad in *TV Times* said: 'So, if you're not an agent and don't want to be left out in the cold, fill in the coupon or phone today for an autumn fashions catalogue.'

It is truly shopping without shops, except that the shop is literally brought into the home – or office – statically yet evocatively. This is done *pictorially* (photography is discussed in Chapter 12); by printing techniques and offset litho which offer great beauty and realism; and by copywriting, which is a very special skill. How well is *your* catalogue written?

Catalogue copywriting excels where sales letter writing so often fails. There are two possible reasons for this. Catalogues have been produced for more than a century, and the limited space available for numerous product descriptions demands concise, precise word-picture writing, with foolproof price details. It is rather like writing captions for photographs: the wording has to say what the picture cannot say for itself. The second reason is that catalogue writing is recognized as copywriting, whereas the majority of sales letter writers indulge in bad business letter writing.

Catalogue copy ranges from the exciting to the factual, according to the product and the marketing. However, as will be shown by the examples quoted later on, exciting copy can degenerate into hyperbole.

ROLE OF THE CATALOGUE

Catalogues can play the following roles:

1   To present merchandise to prospective buyers.
2   To maintain regular mail order sales.
3   To provoke immediate response.
4   To seek retention for future reference and purchase.

Not all catalogues aim to do all four things. Frequency has a bearing on this. Some catalogues are published annually and may well be kept until the next one arrives, while others are issued perhaps quarterly or monthly, replacing the previous one. Then there are seasonal ones like those published by charities. Catalogues of more instant appeal, like those piggybacked on other mailings such as bills, may be very short lived.

CLAIMS IN CATALOGUE COPY

In spite of the excellence of much catalogue copy – and there are some very able and experienced writers – some incredible claims are made in catalogues widely distributed by well-known traders. Some of these claims are manifestly untrue and are offences against the British Code of Advertising Practice. The Advertising Standards Authority, which administers the code, has issued warnings about the claims made in computer trading, especially regarding software.

The ASA has also criticized holiday brochures containing wrong illustrations and inaccurate descriptions, and seven cases were reported in *Case Report* 150 (October 1987). This meant that these complaints from the public were published and quoted in the press, which was poor PR for these culprits. Here are some of them:

Airtours Ltd winter holiday brochure 'included a photograph of apartments which were not the St Julian's apartments . . . claimed that the apartments had "fully equipped kitchens" but the complainant maintained that this was not the case . . . featured a photograph of a sandy beach and details of three places in Malta but the complainant objected that only one of these areas had a sandy beach.' All three complaints were upheld by the ASA.

Blakes Holidays brochure claimed 'a network of beautiful lakes offering 200 cruising miles' but the complainant said that the Broads consisted of less than 130 miles of navigable channel. The ASA upheld the complaint.

Haven Leisure Ltd brochure quoted the price for a seven-person caravan for a week at £81, but the complainant had to pay a £16 supplement for a new caravan although all the caravans of that size were new. The ASA upheld the complaint and was concerned that the holiday was not available at the price quoted.

Thomson Holidays brochure described a 'Cities of Andalucia' tour but the itinerary did not mention that a diversion lasting several hours was made to Torremolinos at the start and close of the tour. The ASA upheld the complaint.

Whether or not you think these are serious or trivial complaints, they could have been avoided.

It may be that errors and false statements occur unintentionally. They may arise through lack of vigilance when writing copy, over-enthusiasm about new lines, inadequate knowledge of products, or naive acceptance of claims made by the manufacturer or supplier.

How does catalogue copy get written? Sometimes, very inefficiently! Foolish assumptions are made that given information is reliable.

How often does the writer ever actually see, touch, use or have any experience of what he is writing about? Rarely. 'Sea view' and 'five minutes from the beach' are legendary fibs of holiday brochures, the products of glib, lazy or optimistic writers.

Many catalogue writers work from buyers' descriptions, or

from sales literature provided by the manufacturer or supplier. It is important to say 'supplier' because many of these products are foreign imports. They come from countries where advertising ethics are unknown and trade descriptions are flaunted, so that it is *your* responsibility to verify claims and evaluate the qualities of such goods. You cannot afford to take anything for granted. If you do you run the risk of being investigated by the ASA, or taken to court under the various consumer protection laws.

Do people who write book club or record club catalogues ever read the books or listen to the records and tapes they describe so effusively? It is physically impossible for them to do more than read, repeat or polish up the blurbs provided by the publishers and record makers.

The Britannia Music catalogues are a laugh a line, but how do serious classical music lovers react to splurges like: 'These radiant and fresh performances from the English Chamber Orchestra are deeply rewarding. Gloriously warm and spaciously conceived, the depth of expression is thoughtfully planned, and Jeffrey Tate leaves us in no doubt that the sound is in the music.' Does the mumbo-jumbo sell records and tapes? Does anyone really bother to read it? More important in these catalogue items are the replica of the record cover, the title of the piece, the composer and the names of the performers plus perhaps a quote from a music magazine. The catalogue writer's hyperbole is irrelevant.

But the origin of catalogue material can be worse than knowing nothing about the product. I once wrote an entire mammoth catalogue from hundreds of buyers' descriptions typed on filing cards. I did so 200 miles away from the company's office in the north of England and never saw one piece of merchandise. At least when I wrote holiday brochures I had been there, and when I write book catalogues I know all the books that are described.

If rapturous descriptions are to be written, the colour pictures should match them. To write 'These bewitchingly beautiful large-flowered bush roses in dazzling colours will be a constant source of delight all summer and autumn long' and to reproduce beside it eight hideous pictures in improbable colours is to insult customers in these days of good printing. But presumably Transatlantic Plastics Ltd got some back street printer in Uzbekistan to print their Smarter Gardens catalogue.

CATALOGUE COPY EXAMPLES

J. Parker, the bulb specialists, have been publishing garden catalogues for decades. Descriptions are terse but lively, for example:

BOTANICAL/ROCKERY TULIPS
Ideal for rockeries or containers, they are the first tulips in flower. They are short with striped and mottled leaves (Greigi or Kaufmannia) and will naturalize, especially the Species varieties. Top size bulbs. Fl. March/April.

Parker's catalogue copy is notably no-nonsense and informative, and the numerous colour pictures are well produced and true to colour.

The Unwin's seed catalogue is one of the best: small, compact, full of beautiful pictures, nicely printed, and packing a fantastic array of gardening lore into some 125 pages. It has quite laid-back product descriptions like this one:

Good King Henry
A versatile perennial vegetable, that deserves to be more widely grown. The leaves are gathered a few at a time, when required, like spinach. The shoots can be blanched and used like asparagus. Sow outdoors April–May and thin to 30 cm/1 ft apart. 5830   69p.

Suttons seed catalogue is another splendid one. The descriptions are brief but helpful, like the following for peas. The reference number and price are in red, which links with the explicit order form where an example is repeated.

19 23 91 ONWARD. Very widely grown in all areas. Heavy crop of blunt-ended pods in pairs containing plump peas. Excellent for tables and freezing, and outstanding for exhibition. Ht approx. 60 cm (2 ft) (*see illustration*). ¼ pt 31E   70p.

Some of the best photography and colour printing is to be found in Bakker's horticultural catalogue. The company operates throughout Europe and has its British office at Sudbury. The catalogues are presumably printed in Holland, which no doubt explains their excellence. The copy, however, is more lyrical than that in most British catalogues. Expressions like 'You should really try it and see it bloom!' and 'No picture can ever do justice to the beauty of this large, globular, scintillating blue flower' or 'You can look forward to exquisite flowers' are very emotive.

To read Bakker Holland's catalogue is not to be offended by effusive language, but to catch the enthusiasm that is endowed with a remarkable vocabulary. The copywriting is brilliant, and a pleasure to read on a dull, wintry day. To prove I am no opponent of direct response marketing, no matter what criticisms I have made in these pages, this catalogue gave great pleasure to my wife and me, and provoked a sizeable order. My only objection was to the free gift gimmicks, which I resented as much as the keys and coins from *Reader's Digest*.

I was impressed by two clever touches. So often with such catalogues the means of reordering (or passing the catalogue on to a friend) are defeated once the order form has been despatched. But Bakker have both a *spare* order form and a *friend's* order form, and these are perforated and detachable. Brilliant!

The personalized address, in the filmwrap envelope, had an extremely appealing reminder (with a picture of Jacques Bakker carrying an armful of red gladioli) that I had not responded to previous mailings. Did this make me feel guilty and anxious to respond? No, but it did encourage me to look at the catalogue. I don't think all those gift gimmicks were necessary. Mr Bakker had enough going for him when the realism of the catalogue was explored.

What do you think? Here is the complete wording:

MR JEFKINS, WILL THIS BE YOUR LAST CATA-
LOGUE, OR MAY I OFFER YOU THESE GLADIOLI
AS A GIFT?

Dear Mr. Jefkins,

To be honest, I really am somewhat worried. Do you know that I have been sending you my catalogues for the past 2 years and have not received an order from you.

Of course, you need not place an order if you're not interested, but sending a catalogue does involve expense, and it would be a pity to make those expenses for somebody who, after all, is not interested.

In that case Mr Jefkins you surely won't mind if I stop sending you my catalogue.

However, if you would still like to receive one, I have some special offers for you.

To start with, you'll receive 15 gladioli free with your order. For extra colour in your garden at 84 Ballards Way.

If you order straight away you'll also receive an exclusive Amsterdam Canal House dating from 1638, in hand-painted ceramic.

And there is still another gift in store for you – a vase with a surprise . . . Plus a credit-card calculator that works on solar power for a give-away price.

Where else would you find so many benefits Mr Jefkins? If I were you I would order quickly. I can assure you that your order will be handled completely to your satisfaction.

With kind regards,

Jacques Bakker

PS Mr Jefkins, I am giving you a 5 year guarantee on all my garden products. That's a 100% certainty of satisfaction.

Free gift gimmicks smack of bazaar trading, of the sort of haggling and offers of special discounts that are to be found among oriental traders. Has their influence infiltrated British direct response marketing? Perhaps it is a reflection of the system of 'recommended prices' and the racket of double pricing (list prices and discounted prices) which has resulted from Harold Macmillan's ending of retail price maintenance. Real prices are obscured by free gifts which have to be paid for, or discounts which merely identify the real price, unless there is some genuine economy in bulk purchases such as carriage costs.

One of our best-known big catalogue firms is Littlewoods. Their descriptions of merchandise (supported by excellent pictures) are very curt and factual, such as:

A   COURT SHOE by Chelsea Cobbler with contrast snake trim in man-made material. Heel height 3½ in approx. Black or red. LC 536 shoes. Sizes 4, 5, 6, 7, 8, £17.99. 20 wks 90p.

Littlewoods seasonal catalogues exceed 1000 pages and are impressive, weighty volumes which place a whole departmental store at your fingertips. The artwork is incredibly realistic. The superb colour photographs do most of the talking and selling, so that the copy for a headboard needs to be only:

J   QUEEN-ANNE-STYLE HEADBOARD. Deeply buttoned. Material: 80% triacetate, nylon. Honey, grey or rose headboard.

Number	To fit bed	Price	20 wks
TH 272	3 ft	£19.99	£1.00
TH 276	4 ft 6 in	£24.99	£1.15
TH 280	5 ft	£28.99	£1.45

Littlewoods catalogues also offer a variety of insurance schemes, and a 12½ per cent discount on purchases is offered as an alternative to the 10 per cent agency commission on sales.

Kays seasonal catalogue of more than 1000 pages also has minimal no-nonsense copy to support excellent full-colour pictures. Two examples from a typical edition are:

5.   SKIRT £9.99
       Single inverted pleat skirt
5   INVERTED PLEATED SKIRT
     Available in a choice of three colours. Length 26 in. Washable. Polyester. Sizes: 12; 14; 16; 18

     EB 7226 Black
     EB 7642 Airforce
     EB 7641 Peach   £9.99. 20 wks 50p.

7   CABIN BED. Has four drawers and large cupboard. Mattress not included (for details of mattress see page 576). Size: 77 × 73 × 26½ in high approximately. Colours: Cream/Brown (01); Cream/Red (02).

*ZB 5969.
£119.99. 20 wks £6.00. 38 wks £3.20.

The absence of an order form, and a seven days a week telephone ordering service, makes home shopping remarkably simple through the K-phone system. In addition to cash price and weekly terms, there are 100-week terms and a Homebuilder credit scheme for the more expensive items, plus a Coverplan insurance scheme as well as other insurance offers.

These big catalogues are models of efficiency and are, of course, based on long experience of selling by post.

What are we to make of some other examples? Let's look at one of those much derided catalogues full of things you never knew you never wanted. From *The Innovations Report* – what a ghastly title – come the following gems of unsubstantiated mummery:

Ultimate driving comfort
Professional drivers, like chauffeurs and taxi drivers the world over, recommend the Massage Mat. It's a great idea for any long-distance driver. Hundreds of polished beads threaded onto strong nylon form around the shape of your back, and allow air between you and the seat. You get a gentle massage as you drive, and you don't get hot and sticky. It fits easily onto any seat, under or over the headrest. Measures 17″ × 54″. Driving Massage Seat. £29.95.

Who are all these 'professional drivers . . . the world over'? The 'testimonial' sounds bogus, although on investigation it proved to be an ingenious Taiwan product. It needs some evidence, such as 'Worn by 50 per cent of Paris taxi drivers'. On a visit to Singapore, the author did find taxi drivers using the Massage Mat. But here's another:

Quartzo
Quartz technology is the secret of this new massager which has medical endorsement. It allows rapid relief from ailments like backache and rheumatic pain. It transmits a series of piezo-electric impulses beneath the skin, which interrupt transmission of the pain message between receptors and the nervous system. It will even stimulate the body's natural painkiller, endomorphin, to give lasting relief. Simple to use, the Quartzo is safe and reliable, and requires no batteries. Quartzo Massager. £59.95.

Well, it is a relief that it requires no batteries. This copy is written in a sort of yuppie gobbledegook which the writer assumes suits readers of the smaller-circulation intellectual newspapers like *The Independent* and *The Observer*. No doubt they understood all that pseudo-medical jargon.

Both the examples from *The Innovations Report* imply testimony, and 'medical endorsement' needs to be specified, not tossed off casually like that. As it stands it defies credibility, and invites scepticism. This is a pity, for Innovations is a reputable firm. Again, on investigation there was medical evidence, but it needed to be made more believable.

Collectibles are a feature of direct response marketing, whether they are coins, medals, pictures and plates or goods bearing a famous name. Norton Collectibles have their catalogues in which the copy is very brief, associated with pictures which really tell most of the story. Here is one item:

FILOFAX
The cult personal organizer finished in black leather handles, all the information a busy executive is likely to need. The filofax also includes a special Norton motorcycle section. Price £43.25.

Charities are also users of direct response marketing. One of the best known, Dr Barnardo's, has a cheerful Christmas gift book from which the following is quoted:

Golf Ball Marker Set. With this easy to use kit you can now avoid fairway confusion by marking your own golf balls with your own personal monogram. A thoughtful gift for the golf starter and pro/ams alike. £7.85.

By a coincidence, the same product appeared in *The Inno-vations Report* mentioned above. It is interesting to compare the different copy used for the same product. Which do you prefer?

<u>Mark your golf balls</u>

No more confusion on the fairways. Simply put the golf ball in the head, squeeze hard and your initials will be printed on the ball. Finished in gold plate, it's supplied with 2 alphabets. A practical and personal gift. Golf Ball Personalizer. £7.95.

This rather more specific and slightly longer copy was enhanced by an excellent 'nut-cracker' view picture, com-pared with the side view in the Dr Barnardo's catalogue.

Wines are yet another product sold by mail order catalogue, and two examples are now quoted. Variously named Selection Gault Millau and Good Wine Selection, this firm uses simple, pleasant catalogues with descriptions such as:

1985 Château Terreblanque, 1er Côtes de Blaye
A wine from an oft forgotten strip of land on the eastern side of the Gironde, now producing wines of real class. Fine drinking now.

Schuler-Wine Ltd produce a more elaborate mailing with a personalized sales letter, a free bottle voucher, and a very promotional pictorial catalogue folder. However, in the midst of all the verbiage and pictures, individual wines are described successfully like this:

The white, crisp and fresh *Gran Vino Bianco*. This medium fruity wine is full of vitality. Serve chilled to accompany fish, poultry and all kinds of seafood.

A formidable mailer is Damart, whose complete shot is worth considering before commenting on the catalogue copy. It arrives every quarter in a see-through plastic film envelope so that there is no doubt who has sent it. The catalogue cover is visible on one side, but the big prize draw is visible on the addressed side. It has all the exuberance of a *Reader's Digest* mailing except that it is much brighter.

Inside we have a lively, full-colour eight-page pictorial tabloid catalogue, foolproof with explicit product inform-ation. There is a two-colour printed sales letter which is too 'printed' to resemble a real letter. The pull-out gimmick reveals a gift voucher for orders within 14 days, prompting action. The big-money prize draw is on the order form – again explicit with its dummy order to demonstrate how to fill it in correctly. A standard postage, packing and insurance charge of 95p seems reasonable. On the reverse of the reply envelope is space to insert the names and addresses of friends to be sent catalogues.

One copy example read:

> H   Driving Gloves. Smart looking and cleverly styled with warm Double Force Thermolactyl. Soft, supple leather palms and inside fingers give excellent steering wheel control. Ventilation holes keep hands dry. How to order – see size chart. Palms: real leather. Backs Thermo-lactyl fabric. Size S, M, L £12.50. Black AGD 3500, Navy AGD 3501, Brown AGD 3503.

The letter H was coded to the picture so that no mistake was possible. This is a useful device found in many pictorial catalogues.

For all its gimmicks and hard selling the Damart catalogue is intelligently produced and provides irresistible armchair shopping. Moreover, if you want to see the merchandise or *feel you could if you wanted to* (which is a confidence booster), addresses are given of 19 strategically located shops.

CHARGING FOR CATALOGUES

Should you make a charge for your catalogues or towards the cost of postage? This poser is not as daft as it seems. So here's another question for you to think about.

While there is magic in the word 'FREE!' complete with screamer – and it rarely fails to win response – a charge will deter time and money wasters like schoolchildren and those who cannot resist writing for anything offered free. Many years ago the holiday business stopped the wastage of guide books on irresponsible applicants by asking for stamps. With British seaside resorts operating on tiny publicity budgets derived from the rates, these stamps were a two-way boon.

It may be that the catalogue is very costly to produce and that a charge is necessary; the charge might be refunded if business results.

Seedsmen and other horticultural suppliers try to reduce wastage by stating in their press advertisements (as Suttons do) that recipients of previous catalogues need not apply again. Others send out postcards to test whether people want the next catalogue, deleting from mailing lists those who do not reply.

Griffon, who advertise their 72-page colour catalogue of wall beds in media such as the *Radio Times*, restrict applications to serious enquirers by asking for a cheque for £4.95 for a copy. At the same time they offer a free colour leaflet.

SPECIALIST CATALOGUES AND MAG-A-LOGS

A comparatively recent development, greatly helped by locational identification of likely customers, is the smaller or special interest catalogue, in contrast to the 'big-book' catalogues of the long-established mail order catalogue firms. They concentrate on lines such as fashion, household or gardening equipment. Some of the famous 'big-book' firms like J. D. Williams now produce A4, A5 or smaller format specialist catalogues of around 16 pages which are targeted at identified markets. Many new firms have arrived who do the same.

Some of these smaller catalogues, sometimes folders or broadsheets, are used for door-to-door distribution or as magazine inserts. Traders as varied as B&Q, Halfords, Tesco and electricity boards use them.

Mag-a-logs or magalogues are an interesting innovation, usually addressed to upmarket readers. There is editorial content plus advertisements which offer goods that can be paid for with charge cards.

TRENDS IN CATALOGUE COPY

A study of scores of catalogues received or obtained while writing this book has shown that the largest, best-established and most successful catalogues contain brief factual copy, often without using a single adjective. Newer catalogues, often promoting non-essentials and novelty products, tend to use more flowery copy. This seems to be contradictory, but catalogue copy addressed to better-off buyers is usually more persuasive or high-pressured than that addressed to working-class buyers. Is the yuppie (young upwardly mobile professional) and woopie (well off older people) market really more gullible, really more susceptible to the banalities of advertising?

Or is it that the newer breed of direct response marketers are as bad at writing catalogue copy as the new breed of financial direct marketers are at writing sales letters? Or maybe they are wrongly advised by agencies which are more familiar with the press advertising of mass market consumer goods? Catalogue copy does need to be credible and convincing, and not merely colourful and compelling.

11   Working with the printer

You are bound to buy print, whether it be sales letters, envelopes, leaflets, folders, price lists, order forms or catalogues, so this is a subject of primary interest in direct response marketing. How much do you know about printing and printers, even if you do use an agency or a direct mail house? It is probably the most expensive part of your promotion. Do you get your money's worth? Here *you* are the customer, the buyer, so good print buying is a major responsibility.

Fortunately, it is a part of your business which you can enjoy and take pride in. Printers are craftsmen with whom it can be a pleasure to work if you take the trouble to co-operate with them. Perhaps I am prejudiced because some of my early training was at the London School of Printing.

Printing has a long history and it is constantly changing, as we have seen in the newspaper world. You can benefit from recent developments. For one thing, the quality of type-setting, papermaking and printing has greatly improved, so that you can have excellent print very economically – colour printing, for example.

Today, print shops range from the huge ones which now do contract printing for national newspapers to compact units, often with design studios. But printers still tend to specialize in certain classes of print, and you need to find printers best capable of producing your kind of work.

It pays to talk to printers, and not just to print salesmen, and to visit them, see their plants and discuss your work with them. A lot depends on the kind of machines they have, and the extent to which they have typesetting, folding, binding, laminating and other facilities and do not have to farm out parts of the work to outside specialists.

QUOTATIONS

The first step is to invite quotations, and you will be surprised how they differ. Price variations may result from the way you have described your requirements, but may also depend on what kind of equipment printers have.

When seeking quotations you should be precise about what you want, and give the printer the fullest information about the job. What quantity, how many colours, what kind and weight of paper, how many pictures, how much copy, what size page, how many pages, what sort of binding, how many and what kind of folds, and what delivery date do you want? Some of these things you may not know or understand, and that is why it is sensible to talk to printers. They will advise, and a good printer will volunteer ideas or suggest alternatives.

At the time of wanting to know the printing costs you may have written nothing, obtained no pictures, and prepared no layout. But at least you can make a dummy, estimate the number of pictures and words, and know the general shape and size of the piece of print. Ideally, you should be able to give the printer a rough layout and indicate picture areas and the volume of wording. You can photocopy this dummy and send it to different printers so that they can give you quotations.

One thing to remember when you later send the complete copy to the chosen printer: be sure all the wording is finalized. It can be very costly to make numerous amendments or rewrite if, when you see the proofs, you don't like what was written. The only corrections to proofs should be of the printer's errors in typesetting, spacing and positioning. Layout and copy should resemble an architect's drawing and a quantity surveyor's specifications. Once again, it pays to visit a printer and talk to him so that you are both absolutely clear about the job.

In a short chapter it is not possible to deal with such a subject in great depth, but there are some particular aspects of printing which are worth special attention. One of these is typography.

TYPOGRAPHY

The appearance and legibility of your print is an important facet of communication. It is well worth while taking an interest in typography rather than just leaving it to the printer, although his advice should be sought. You need to know what typefaces he has.

Typography is the art of specifying the style and size of type to turn your wording into print. There is all the difference between typewritten copy and printed copy.

There are hundreds of different typefaces. Roughly, they fall into two groups: display and text. There are also sanserif and serif faces, the first having no short horizontal lines at the top and bottom or ends of strokes. If more than one design of typeface is used, there should be a harmonious blend.

Printers have a selection of typefaces, although not always the same or as large a selection as others. Certain popular typefaces like Times are held by most printers. You should ask printers to let you have a copy of their type specimens manual. This will show you the variety of typefaces they have, usually set out in roman, italic and different weight versions (by 'weight' is meant the lightness or boldness of the type). You can then make comparisons and your choice.

You will notice that some types allow more or fewer characters to the line, and this can determine how many words can be set in a given space. There will be differences in x-height, that is the height of small letters like 'a' and 'o'. Some of the more decorative types have low x-heights, which makes them less easy to read in small sizes.

A lot of promotional print is set throughout in sanserif – for both display lines and panels or columns of text. This is a lazy habit, originating from the small selection of typefaces that used to be available for phototypesetting by litho printers. Sanserif faces give bold displays, but are less legible for small text. Books are not set in sanserif. And if shiny paper is used, sanserif faces are often less easy to read than those with serifs, which are known as text or book faces. But a blend of sanserif display lines and serif text can make effective contrast.

A designer who specifies sanserif type throughout a job is

either ignorant of typography, or out of date and unaware of the increase in typeface availability among phototypesetters. If print is being designed for you, make sure you check and approve the typefaces being specified. A lot of customers don't; they put up with slipshod typography, and fail to realize that they are sacrificing a vital tool of communication.

There are many beautiful typefaces, and your print can be given character, legibility and readability if you choose carefully.

But don't spoil your print by using devices which decrease legibility. It may be dramatic or give emphasis if you print small areas such as display lines on a colour background, but don't use such a heavy colour that it kills the words.

Similarly, beware of reversing words to read white on a black or coloured background. This may be all right for the occasional display panel with a few large words, but small text can be lost if reversed. It may be a pretty design idea, but it can destroy readability. Beware of designers who think in terms of shapes to look at rather than words to read.

Another way to achieve readability is to be generous with white space. Space between lines of copy, space round copy, good margins, and indented paragraphs all help to make your message readable. A free (unjustified) right-hand edge does not help readability; it is a hangover from the days when IBM settings could not be justified and had to have ragged right-hand edges.

Short paragraphs have a similar effect. Don't bore a reader with great slabs of wording. This may mean writing shorter, crisper copy to let some daylight into the layout. Or it may permit the use of larger type. Short paragraphs, short sentences and short words help to speed up the reading.

It is worth studying catalogues to see how often or seldom the above principles of good typography are practised. Sadly they seldom are, because designers too often usurp the role of typographers. So much nicely designed, nicely printed, well-written print is ruined by bad typography which merely plants a volume of words in a given space. Whether it is legible and readable never enters the heads of those designers who never read but only look.

An example is the classy-looking Kitchens Direct catalogue, which has long narrow panels of some 180 words of copy set in small sanserif type on shiny paper. The copy has short lines, it is unjustified, and paragraphs (if recognizable as such) are not indented and have no space between them; these are three offences against legibility. Such silly setting seems anxious to prevent the reader from being able to read it. But these malpractices are common. Designers, printers and their clients don't even notice these foolish faults: the customer is left to struggle to read badly set copy. They don't have to in newspapers, magazines and books, so why should they in your print? Surely, sales print should be even clearer to read!

On the other hand, the beautifully produced 300-page brochure from English Country Cottages is packed with colour pictures and descriptions of scores of properties. The copy has to be set small, but it is set in readable serif type with indented paragraphs.

Typography has been emphasized here because it is the means of communicating quickly, clearly and effectively. This will not be obvious when you look at words produced on a typewriter. You have to think how best will this typescript appear in print. You may even find it helpful to have a little copy set in different typefaces to see how these samples compare.

LASER PRINTING

There are many laser printing machines, such as the IBM 3800, the Xerox range, the Mercurian SSI, the Siemans and the Canon. Of these the IBM 3800 is probably the most widely used.

Laser printing makes it possible to enliven mail shots such as sales letters with special effects like personalization within the text of a letter, unusual layouts, or combinations of different typefaces. Different machines permit sheet feed or continuous feed. Laser printing can be applied to personalized reply cards, prize draw certificates, invoices and other print apart from sales letters. The names, figures, choice of typeface and so on are controlled by computer.

Companies like Crawfords Computing of Liverpool and Imagen of London supply detailed booklets setting out the range of work that can be laser printed, and in particular specifying the paper requirements which are essential for this kind of imaginative printing.

PRODUCTION SCHEDULE

Yours is not the only job a printer has to handle, nor is it the only task for which you or your agent is responsible. If print work is to be carried out efficiently, timetables are involved. Delays can involve extra costs.

It is therefore wise to agree a production schedule with your printer, and then see that you both keep to it. Printers, especially their sales representatives, tend to be optimistic about delivery dates. Make sure your required delivery date is well before you need it, particularly if your print has to be delivered to another firm which is handling the mailing, insertion or door-to-door distribution. If you tell a printer you want a job a week earlier than you really do, it may arrive on time.

A simple production schedule can follow this pattern, the D-day numbers in this example covering a month:

Production schedule

Copy to printer	D−30
Proofs from printer	D−20
Corrected proofs to printer	D−17
Delivery by printer	D-day

This can be elaborated according to the complexities of the job. It may be necessary to allow for revised proofs and a final OK, or colour proofs may have to be checked for accuracy of colour. The printer may be responsible for packing and posting, or inserts may have to be delivered to publishers' printers by certain dates. Dates need to be fixed to suit the printer's workload and your own planning for mailing, media advertising or mail drop.

PROOF-READING

Reading proofs is a chore, but it is your responsibility, not the printer's, to see that the job is correctly laid out with the right pictures and captions in place, and that the wording is set correctly. If there is not vigilance on your part it is easy for errors to slip through. There can be wrong typefaces, sizes or weights, or the spacing or positioning can be improved. Wrong captions may appear under pictures. A picture can be upside down or the wrong way round. In litho printing, everything is pasted down, and it may be pasted in the wrong place, not centred or without proper spacing. Adjustments are easily made *before* plate-making, that is when you are shown a photocopy of the artwork from which the printing plate will be made.

Because you know what you want to see, it is easy to read into proofs what you expect to find and so overlook mistakes. Modern computerized phototypesetting is very accurate, but a small mistake in, say, a price can ruin your work and cause problems with customers. Proofs must therefore be read slowly, syllable by syllable, and then reread; it is often a good idea to ask a stranger to the job to also read the proofs. It is surprising how two proof-readers will spot completely different errors!

But do not rewrite proofs: 'author's corrections', as distinct from printer's errors, can be costly and may cause delayed delivery. Get it right *before* you send copy to the printer. Don't wait to see what it looks like when proofed. This warning is worth repeating because so many print customers never know what they really want until they see what they don't want. Then they wonder why the job turns out to be more expensive than they anticipated. This is a form of budgetary control – or common sense.

DESKTOP PUBLISHING

The computer has made possible the writing, editing, layout and typography of publications and on-line transmission direct to the printer. This is quite well established for house journal production, but the same techniques can be applied to the production of catalogues. You may find this well worth looking into, especially with work that can be repeated with updates, since the original material can be stored on disc.

One such method is the Wordsmith Publishing System, which uses the Apple Mackintosh microcomputer and costs about £10 000 including software and laser printer. This system is designed to output direct to Linotron 500, 300 and 100 typesetters via an electronic link with the printer. Fonts, leading (spaces between material) and computer-generated graphics can be set direct on paper sizes up to A3. The actual page make-up software can produce full-colour separations as well as display on the screen of the colours used. Drafts of work can be produced in full colour on a matrix printer or in higher resolution (black and white only) on the Laserwriter. The Wordsmith system can be installed by Appletek of London.

12   Working with the photographer

Pictures which are too clever, too professional, too unnatural or unrealistic may lack conviction. Do the models in your catalogues, brochures or off-the-page promotions look like Page Three girls, or like you, your sister, your girlfriend or your mother-in-law? If customers cannot picture themselves using the sunbed or pushing the lawnmower, dining in the restaurant or wearing the dress, they may not think the goods are meant for them. To look at some travel brochures you would think no one over 20 went on holiday or on cruises!

Perhaps you think that is an exaggeration – that you should sell dreams even when promoting a natty line of clothes pegs. But glamorization can go too far. It can be the end of the sales pitch. Not always, of course. There can be appeals to vanity when an older woman may want to emulate a younger one. You will be wise to study the psychology of using apt models. A dress may make a fat model look thinner!

The art of using photography effectively is to remember that the camera is a means of conveying a message, just like the voice, pen, brush, typewriter or word processor.

Photographers are like artists: they specialize in certain mediums or subjects. You may need one who specializes in, say, fashion, table-top, outdoor scenes, interiors, flowers or children.

Some photographers are fairly versatile, but others are much better at taking one kind of picture than another. It may be a matter of equipment – make of camera, possession of a studio or of special lighting equipment. Another question is delivery: some photographers will give you contacts next day, others will take a fortnight. What is your deadline for prints or transparencies?

Good photography depends as much on your ability to work with the photographer as with your choice of photographer. A professional photographer knows the technicalities and techniques of his trade, but he does not know what you want unless you tell him. That means you must know what you do want. You should not just call in a photographer and expect him to get on with the job as you might a plumber when you have a burst pipe.

Photography is a matter of story-telling with a camera, not merely the taking of record shots. And yours is the story to be told, not the photographer's. Each picture has to be planned. You are the director, as when a film is made. Did you see that television programme which showed how lovingly David Lean directed the camera during the filming of 'A Passage To India'?

So, what precisely do *you* want to say? Do you *know*? Have you thought it out, picture by picture, throughout the piece of print? A photographer may think 'this is a nice angle' or 'this lighting effect will be dramatic', and his artistic ideas can be totally irrelevant. Of course, if you use the same photographer a number of times he will become familiar with the type of pictures you want. He may well offer valuable advice. Between you, you may have perfected a drill. That is excellent, but it has to begin with you.

For instance, suppose you are producing a brochure for a conference centre. You will know what conference organizers are looking for, and how best your particular facilities can satisfy their needs. The impressive exterior of your hall may be less important than the audiovisual equipment or effects you have installed. A view of the kitchen may be less important than a thousand delegates eating. You need to assess your qualities from a pictorial standpoint. An empty auditorium or stage, a blank screen or inactive reception area can make the place look as if it is up for sale. You have to see pictures with the eyes of the eventual beholder.

Try to visualize the pictures which will influence decisions. You have to produce a shooting script.

But equally a selection of jewellery, or the stamps to be auctioned, or your range of fitted kitchens, need to be portrayed in certain ways if they are going to produce action. How? That is your decision, not the photographer's.

Every picture needs to be planned in two ways:

1   With a written brief, which will resemble the stage directions for a play or the shooting script for a film or video.

2   With a rough sketch of the composition of the picture. The composition will angle the picture to show what is most significant – the control knob, the large windows, the safety device, the immaculate head waiter or whatever it may be.

Composition is the secret of good photography. Think how dramatically Rembrandt made use of patches of light. Composition is all-important. Take a single subject such as a clock. Shall it be photographed face-on and flat, or turned slightly to give a three-dimensional effect? If the latter, which is usually preferable, shall it be turned to the left or the right? The choice can be important when photographing, say, a camera or a sewing machine if some essential feature is on one side or another.

If you are taking photographs to fit a layout of a page, pictures on the left of the page should be looking inwards, and vice versa. Not every subject can be reversed if an existing picture is being used which is looking the wrong way. This applies to people in pictures too. The reader's eye will follow the direction presented to him by a picture, and you don't want the reader's attention wandering off the page. In which direction are the eyes looking?

You don't have to make do with given pictures if you plan in advance exactly what you want.

If you are using *colour* pictures make sure they *are* colour pictures. Subjects like flowers or fashions, book jackets or butterflies are usually colourful, but most subjects or scenes are made up of dull greys, blues, mauves, browns and greens. Yellow, orange and red are often absent. Somehow, these bright colours need to be introduced. Dull colours make a picture recede from the eye, while bold bright colours bring a picture forward. Black and yellow or black and orange are very striking combinations.

But with black and white pictures, lighting effects, shadows and silhouettes produce dramatic effects, plus contrasts between black and white.

These differences can be observed by comparing black and white with colour films in the cinema or on television.

PEOPLE IN PICTURES

People can add realism and enhance the interest of some pictures, but they can be irrelevant and distracting in others. 'People' usually mean models and model fees, unless pictures can be peopled by the general public, customers or employees. Scenes may include customers, but a hotel or restaurant scene can be peopled by members of the owner's family or staff. For the conference pictures mentioned earlier, photographs can be taken while an event is in progress.

We are gregarious animals. People do like looking at other people, whether it be a famous personality who is giving a testimonial, an attractive model, or a model representing a typical user with whom the reader can relate.

Choice of appropriate model invites several considerations. Do you want a recognizable person like Lulu in the Freeman's ads, someone who glamorizes the product; or do you want someone who looks natural, homely or 'right' for the subject? Do you want to give your mail shot an air of femininity, manliness, class, youthfulness, cheerfulness, seriousness or modernity?

Will customers be put off by a model who is nothing like them, or will they be tempted to look at all the pretty models and ignore the goods? Maybe fashion goods will make buyers feel good if they wear clothes like those the youthful models are wearing. But such a model will look stupid if you are selling annuities. These considerations do not always seem to have bothered some of the compilers of certain mail order catalogues.

What the person is doing in the picture can also be important. It may be better to have a rear or side view of a person using a computer so that the screen is visible. For products like rings or wrist-watches, only fingers or wrists need to be photographed. You will have to choose a model with the right features, hands or arms, and it may not matter whether they are tall, short, thin or fat.

Correct clothing is yet another consideration. We see some oddly dressed people mowing lawns, decorating walls and even using cake mixers. Sometimes it looks as if the same model has simply moved from one subject to another while still wearing the same clothes. So watch the 'wardrobe' aspects if you want credible pictures.

SIZE OF OBJECTS

Do your pictures demonstrate the size of products, and is it an advantage that they do? Very easily, a photograph can give a false impression of size if the product is not associated with something of known size. Size can be indicated when a small object is placed in the palm of the hand, or held in the fingers, or set beside a familiar object. Tall or large subjects can be associated with the human figure to indicate their height or bulk.

★   ★   ★

Your particular subject may call for other techniques. Use or enjoyment can be presented pictorially, such as by the sniffing Bisto kids. If it is a comfortable chair, have someone really relaxing in it. If it is easy to use, show how easily it can be operated. A picture can be more convincing than words.

13   Electronic media

Under electronic media we shall consider radio, television, telephone, electronic mail, audio tapes and video tapes as they apply to direct response marketing.

TELEMARKETING

This is a medium which requires the respondent or customer to have or have access to the telephone. The Post Office claims that compared with the next most personal medium, direct mail, the telephone can be from three to six times more effective. In the USA the telephone is the largest direct response medium, with expenditure running at about $34b a year. There are 1300 American direct response agencies and thousands of in-house units, employing 300 000 people.

In Britain, telephone capacity has more than doubled in recent years, so that access is widespread and resistance to telephone selling has lessened. There are some 100 specialist telephone marketing agencies in Britain, a sample of these services being described later in this chapter. Between £50m and £60m a year is spent on telemarketing in Britain, and the market has trebled in recent years and continues to grow. It is expected to grow at a rate of 50 per cent over the next five years. According to a study made by the British Direct Marketing Association in 1987, more than 500 000 staff, working in 150 000 to 160 000 UK companies, are solely or mainly responsible for handling inbound enquiries or orders.

This is a medium with very special advantages, but it can have its problems too. It has been used very successfully to sell insurance, magazine subscriptions, advertisement space, retail goods, office equipment, real estate, theatre seats, conferences and seminars, and for executive search.

Let us analyse some of the pros and cons, bearing in mind that telephone selling can work both ways. Calls can be initiated by both *seller* (outbound) and *buyer* (inbound). The first uses a call list; the second responds to direct mail, off-the-page promotions or door-to-door distributions.

ADVANTAGES OF TELEMARKETING

1 Uniform sales messages can be made in advance so that calls can be kept as short as possible, and the desired message can be delivered.

2 It can be tested by measuring the response to different versions of the sales message.

3 Unlike print – which is fixed once it is produced – telephone messages can be adjusted according to experience.

4 A telemarketing campaign can be mounted quickly, and you don't have to spend perhaps weeks on producing print or preparing and placing advertisements. This is ideal for urgent campaigns. You may need to sell something quickly for cash flow purposes, or because orders are slow. You may need to sell vacant seats or unsold advertisement space.

5 It can supplement direct response advertising in other media such as TV, radio and cinema commercials, press advertisements, outdoor posters and Underground posters, car cards, direct mail, mail drops and other media such as Prestel.

6 It is personal and interactive. You can answer questions and overcome objections, and also remove the inertia which static media have difficulty in combating. Printed material can be put aside for a decision on another day, but during a telephone conversation you can produce a definite response. It can also effect an agreed follow-up if an immediate decision cannot be taken.

7 It can motivate positive inbound response, as when an off-the-page advertisement produces telephone enquiries or, better still, orders. The Post Office offers a telephone

TAN service for handling inbound calls, receiving calls in your name and forwarding the information on a daily, weekly or monthly basis. This can relieve you of having to 'man' a telephone to deal with response, or finding the extra number of incoming calls impossible to handle. Ask yourself this: when you give a telephone number in your advertising, can you cope with the dozens, hundreds or thousands of calls the advertisement may generate? Consider, for instance, the possible response from an advertisement in either *TV Times* or *Radio Times* with their multimillion circulations.

8 For fulfilment purposes, inbound calls can be directed to the source for distribution of samples, brochures, application forms and other items offered in advertisements. The Post Office telephone TAN service can effect distribution within 24 hours, which is days or weeks faster than the reader service schemes operated by publishers. Turnround of enquiries is important, otherwise applicants may have lost interest or bought something else if there is a delay.

9 To pick up a telephone and dial an enquiry or order is less trouble than having to mail it, and a quicker reply can be expected. Again, the inertia bug is overcome. Business people nowadays make more telephone calls than they write letters. You can exploit this habit.

10 A telephone call enjoys solus rating in that it competes with no other advertising for attention.

11 When the telephone rings people usually answer it, and you have won instant attention.

DISADVANTAGES OF TELEMARKETING

1 Unless you or your staff can handle either outbound or inbound calls, telemarketing is not for you. It is useless if you cannot have the staff, the trained staff, available and able to do the job as a continuous operation. Equally, it is useless if you are not organized, internally or externally, to receive and handle calls at any time. Callers will be put off if you are engaged and do not answer, and they seldom like answerphones.

2   They may resent unsolicited phone calls of a selling nature even more than they resent unsolicited junk mail. The American method of cold calling by dialling at random, by means of a computer, until there is an answer, is an intrusive method frowned upon in this country. Nevertheless, a version of this (even without a computer) is used by some salesmen.

3   The call may be inconvenient. People may be in the bath, having a meal, watching television, or busy in the office. Skill in timing calls is required. The ploy that the caller 'has a representative in the district' is disliked. So, too, is the fake market research survey approach. Telemarketing has been abused by those who try to be too clever. Unwelcome calls are self-defeating.

4   The caller is invisible and a stranger, unlike a face-to-face salesman. One accepts that the writer of a sales letter is a stranger, or that the writer of sales literature is anonymous. However, a disembodied voice makes great strains on the credibility or likeableness of the speaker. A too persuasive voice can be off-putting, a charming voice may sound too insincerely flattering. A telephone salesman's voice can lack the acceptability and authenticity of a radio voice, whether newsreader, presenter or actor.

5   It is expensive if outbound calls do not produce cost-effective results. Space salesmen and women often call people whose advertisements they have seen in other papers. Surely they must realize that advertising is planned, budgeted and booked a long time in advance, and that there is rarely additional money to allocate to other media? Such telemarketing is often too late.

6   Telemarketing is more difficult and different in Britain than in America, where the telephone has been a way of life for so long. Here, a 'telephone culture' has yet to be created, and prejudices about the telephone have yet to be reconciled. There are still many people who resent the telephone bell as an invasion of their privacy.

7   The inefficiencies of British Telecom do not always encourage confidence in the system. Lines are inoperative

far too long, and crossed lines are such a constant
irritation.

8   It has been difficult to impose a code of practice on
telemarketing because there are so many in-house
amateurs or ordinary field salesmen who are untrained.
They give the medium a bad name by their bungling,
intrusive and over-persuasive tactics. The British Direct
Marketing Association has made efforts to provide guidelines, but they can apply only to their own members.
However, the BDMS guidelines make enlightening
reading (see Chapter 17).

Clear-cut rules control the selling of investments over
the telephone, and unauthorized practitioners are banned
from making unsolicited calls, except for life insurance
companies and unit trusts. Even then, the prospect must
have expressed willingness to be phoned.

It is not always realized that it has long been held
unethical to call on enquirers who have asked for sales
literature. Some advertisers make the mistake of asking
for a telephone number without giving the respondent the
option of inviting or refusing a personal visit. The only
remedy for the alert applicant is for him not to give a
telephone number! Unsolicited home visits are banned by
the British Code of Advertising Practice, and an unsolicited phone call can be equally undesirable.

*   *   *

From the above analysis it will be seen that there are pros and
cons in plenty! There are also big distinctions between
outbound and inbound calls, which are qualified by the first
being unsolicited and the second being voluntary.

SPECIAL USES OF TELEMARKETING

Some uses have already been described. However here is a list,
adapted from one presented by British Telecom Telephone
Marketing Services:

List building/updating From either outbound or inbound calls, data can be obtained on names, addresses, job titles and job functions in order to build or update mailing lists and databases.

Lead screening Calls can identify good prospects before mailing a prospect list.

Lead generation and qualification Following up leads generated by advertising by asking questions to see whether they justify fuller following up, or to discover what they are particularly interested in. For instance, reader service enquiries.

Handling fulfilment Receiving requests for items offered in advertisements, and distributing them, such as brochures.

Closing sales Accepting orders and credit card payments by telephone.

Upgrading or up-selling and cross-selling customers Phoning existing customers and selling them additional or new lines.

Location search/appointment setting Advising enquirers of their nearest supplier, or making appointments for salesmen to call if an enquirer when returning a coupon has expressed willingness to be called on.

Generating attendance Asking prospects to attend events such as conferences, seminars, courses, exhibitions, fashion shows, demonstrations, including following up invitations which have not yet produced response.

Customer service Ringing customers who have not ordered recently, handling enquiries and replying to complaints.

Generating traffic For example, encouraging retailers to visit wholesalers, inviting customers to demonstrations or store events.

Sampling programmes Inviting prospects to accept samples.

Lapsed accounts Reactivating old customers, or renewing memberships and subscriptions.

Research Telephone surveys can be conducted quickly, either by appointment or spontaneously.

Messaging Using a service to receive messages.

Sales promotion Handling response to competitions and phone-ins rather than mail-in premium and incentive schemes.

Fund-raising   Contacting prospective or regular donors to raise funds, increase size of donations or reactivate lapsed supporters.

This list shows the versatility of telemarketing, and it may suggest some uses which had not previously occurred to you. You may even be surprised that there are so many opportunities to use the telephone as a promotional medium.

FREEFONE

Inbound response can be induced by giving prospects a Freefone facility in off-the-page advertisements, sales letters, catalogues and sales literature. It is a courtesy as well as an inducement, and creates goodwill. The magic word 'Free' is exploited, and so that is extra persuasion and yet at the same time has the PR aspect of establishing good customer relations.

However, Freefone is a lot more expensive than Freepost, and can be very costly if it invites frivolous or unprofitable calls. One of the best uses is where you want to have the opportunity to talk to interested clients, discuss points and answer questions, and secure a sale.

At the time of writing Freefone has 6000 clients. The cost is linked to operator charges, with an initial fee of £250, a quarterly rental of £20, and calls at operator rate plus 25p a call service charge. That means an average cost of £1.45 a call for the advertiser, which is not cheap. If the price of the product or service is high, such as with a holiday tour or an insurance policy, the cost can be swallowed, but it can be a prohibitive on-cost for smaller priced goods like packets of garden seeds. An advantage is that the caller has to remember only words and not numbers.

LINKLINE (0800)

One of the advantages of having an 0800 number is its memorability. However, it is less simple than the Freefone; compare 'Freefone Real Fires' for British Coal with Volvo's 0800 400 430 and Prudential Holborn's 0800 010 345, although TWA's 0800 22 2222 is highly memorable. Looking through direct response and other consumer ads in magazines like the *Radio Times* and the weekend colour magazines, Linkline numbers predominate as a free telephone facility, and Linkline has tended to take over from Freefone since its introduction in 1985. But most advertisers prefer to give their own phone number and expect the prospect to pay for the call.

Linkline has a connection charge of £250 for each line, plus a quarterly rental charge of £100. Each call is charged at its regular peak, standard or cheap rate per minute. For a large number of inbound calls it is more cost-effective than Freefone, and it suits users like Saga Holidays who could be phoned at any time. In their advertisements Saga picture a telephone receiver and print the word 'free' in bold type. Their Linkline number is 0800 300 600, which is easy to remember.

TELEDATA (200 0 200)

While prominence has been given to BT services we should not forget another system made famous by the memorable Teledata numbers 200 0 200. Teledata is a subsidiary of Air Call. Ninety per cent of its £2m business comes from inbound calls. That magic number was originally bought from a Colindale solicitor for £100 and a crate of champagne!

The invitation to ring 200 0 200 to make an enquiry or give an order is not only convenient but convincing because of the familiarity of the number. It is rather like the 999 emergency number.

Teledata also operates an outbound telephone marketing service. Using an American software system, Teledata can provide customer-specific scripts for promotional campaigns. For example when 200 0 200 enquiries are generated by press advertising it is possible for Teledata not only to receive enquiries but to convert them into immediate follow-ups instead of simply forwarding enquiries to the client. Enquirers to motor-car advertisements have been converted into appointments for test drives.

A large-scale use of both the Linkline 0800 and Teledata 200 0 200 systems for inbound calls was during the various flotations of privatized enterprises such as BT, TSB, British Gas and BP, when names and addresses were collected of people wanting prospectuses.

SPECIAL AGENCY SERVICES

Because telemarketing is time consuming, requires trained telephonists, needs a number of available lines, can be a 24-hour operation, and often must be handled quickly over a short period, a number of specialist services exist.

We have drawn on information from British Telecom Telephone Marketing Services, which services about 20 per cent of the market. There are also numerous private services, a sample of which are now discussed.

Agency costs include a set-up fee, a monthly administration charge, the BT telephone bill and a fee per call. The economies of this depend on whether a company has equal facilities, and whether it is a short-term, occasional or regular operation. In most cases, a telemarketing agency offers a valuable 'third arm'. Many of these agencies offer similar services to those in the earlier list of special uses of telemarketing.

Companies which offer these omnibus services are Directline Telemarketing of London, Salestalk Ltd of London, Teleproms of Burnham, Prowess Marketing Ltd of Manchester, Knight Sales and Marketing Ltd of Maidstone, and Golly Slater Telephone Marketing of Cardiff. Phonesell of London was founded by Pauline Marks, who pioneered telemarketing in the UK and wrote the book *The Telephone Marketing Book*.

Some of these agencies offer particular services. For example, Prowess Marketing has a very wide choice of services which range from recruitment screening to retail stock checking. Phonesell offer an extra 120-line availability using a premium rated network. Availability of telephone lines is a characteristic of these agencies. Answering Ltd, who specialize in customer service and incoming call fulfilment (mainly for executive search), maintain 1000 lines. The Pauline Marks organization has 30 operators plus 60 other staff, keeps 170 lines in regular use, and handles all kinds of direct response services for clients like British Rail, De Beers, Canada Life, Leyland, MK and Tobler. Most of them operate on a telephone-hour basis.

ELECTRONIC MAIL

Electronic mail boxes linked to personal computers are commonplace in many large companies, often operating across continents or the globe. Another Royal Mail service is Intelpost, which can direct messages to facsimile, telex or micro users. Intelpost offers a fast service, and items can be handed in to 114 UK centres and transmitted to 30 countries. While this is intended mainly for single messages, it can be adapted to transmitting urgent sales messages to a limited or very specialized list of prospects, whether or not you or they have electronic equipment. It is a very flexible system indeed for making rapid offers to selected buyers.

The Telecom Gold electronic mail box service is based on a large computer centre in London. If you and your customers have existing terminals such as a microcomputer, word processor or VDU, it is possible to communicate between work spaces by telephone. Telecom Gold was set up in 1981 to market the ITT Dealcom service on behalf of British Telecom. An A4 letter can be distributed from a word processor to any number of UK destinations for less than the price of a stamp. For only 30p more, 50 copies could be sent to Hong Kong! Through the Telecom Gold system you can also contact any Telex subscriber.

For £7.50 you can obtain a 19 minute video 'Electronic Mail has Arrived' from Telecom Gold Ltd, 60–68 St Thomas Street, London SE1 3QU. It can be ordered by Access or Visa on 01 403 6777.

RADIO AND TELEVISION

Commercials on independent local radio stations can stimulate enquiries by giving telephone numbers and producing inbound calls. These may use actual numbers of the Freefone, Linkline or Teledata facilities already described.

Much depends on the type of audience and time of day. Listeners at home or at work can easily write down telephone numbers, but this is less easy when listening to a car radio. A greater variety of opportunities occurs with television. Again, telephone numbers can be used, they can appear on screen, calls can be serviced by the television station, and orders and credit card numbers can be phoned in to a computer ordering service. Television stations will then process print-outs to advertisers, usually within 24 hours. Record companies like K-Tel sell records in this way.

Television commercials can also be linked to magazines like *TV Times* or newspapers in which more detailed advertisements with coupons are inserted. This is a method often used by holiday and travel firms. It can be regionalized through selected ITV stations and regional editions of *TV Times* or local newspapers.

Videotext or viewdata and teletext information systems on the ITV Oracle and Telecom Prestel systems can be used in direct marketing. On Oracle, commercial pages can be broadcast, and they can be 'flagged' on popular pages such as news items. Prestel still tends to have small domestic usage, but can be useful for business-to-business marketing.

TELEX AND FAX

Sales letters in telex form can be used in business-to-business marketing where customers have telex numbers. This medium has the merit of urgency since telex messages demand immediate attention. Telex messages have been used to seek attendances at conferences, and telex lends itself admirably to international conferences when messages can be transmitted more quickly than by mail. Facsimile machines are taking over from telex, and can also be used to transmit sales messages to companies with fax facilities, especially in business-to-business trading.

ADMAIL

While this Post Office redirection service can apply to direct mail, press, radio or TV advertising, it is particularly useful with broadcast media, and it can be combined with Freepost. It allows you to give a short, easy-to-remember address, and the Post Office will redirect replies to you or your fulfilment house.

14 Off-the-page selling and inserts

Mail order traders have long used press advertising to sell goods by post, and many of them have been and still are small and even one-man businesses. They have been encouraged by publishers eager to sell space, but at the same time the more reputable publishers have sought to avoid complaints from readers, and to vet advertisers.

I once served on an advisory committee set up by a multimillion circulation family magazine. Two problems had to be confronted. There were unscrupulous advertisers who attempted to foist useless or undesirable products on the public. There were also potential advertisers who did not appreciate the immense pulling power of mail order advertisements, and had neither sufficient stocks nor the ability to handle a huge volume of orders in a short time. I was also at one time responsible for the predecessor to the Advertising Standards Authority and, in particular, it was incredible how disreputable firms tried to sell dubious 'cures' and treatments by mail. One firm supplied an outline drawing of the human body on which the sufferer marked where it hurt!

Today, there is not only legislation like the new Consumer Protection Act 1987 and many other Acts, but the MOPS and other schemes operated by the press, the British Code of Advertising Practice administered by the Advertising Standards Authority, *Which?* reports, the precautionary 'allow 28 days for delivery' proviso in many off-the-page direct response advertisements, and the code and guidelines of the British Direct Marketing Association. In numerous ways, which are described in Chapter 17, the consumer is well protected. The direct response marketer needs to be well aware of voluntary and legal controls when conducting advertising. It is a truism that there is nothing wrong with advertising, only with advertisers.

So make sure you are familiar with both legal and voluntary controls.

Deception may not be intentional, but you do have to be careful not to make ambiguous claims, however innocently. An oldie from the past was to use the expression 'art silk' without a full point after 'art', so that what was really rayon could be misconstrued to mean art and not artificial silk. Another one was to refer to raincoats or watches as waterproof when they were no more than water resistant.

These comments are made in advance of Chapter 17 because print media advertising is liable to be scrutinized critically by publishers, the ASA and the public. In preparing copy it is vital to write product descriptions and to make claims which are beyond reproach. Direct response advertisement copy has to achieve immediate response, and by its very nature it has to be more hard selling than other advertising where the response is at the point of sale, goods can be inspected and buying decisions can be made more deliberately and leisurely.

To buy clothes, tableware or furniture without prior examination demands great confidence in the supplier. Such faith is inspired partly by the corporate image of the advertiser but principally by the wording of the advertisement and by its illustrations. There is always the danger that people will read into advertisements what they want to read, basing their interpretations on preconceived notions.

For example, one well-known firm offered a free gift of a cut glass vase, and pictured it holding flowers. It was easy for a reader to think in terms of the average vase standing maybe nine inches tall, and perhaps not noticing that the free gift was only three inches tall or about the height of a salt cellar. (The measurement was in a paragraph of 60 words.) You do have to try to think the way your reader may think. It is no good blaming the reader for making mistakes.

Again, if you are selling knock-down furniture or other goods which have to be assembled, it is necessary to explain that it does have to be put together. Some people are baffled by such assemblies. One advertised wardrobe needed a power drill to build it. Advertisements usually show a product already erected, not flat or in its parts. Customers buy the article as *shown*, not a kit. They may not have even a Philips screwdriver. You must take nothing for granted – otherwise you will be parodied by television comedians as MFI have been.

Some mail order goods are once-only buys, but you may aim to build live customer lists and gain repeat business. Only satisfied customers come back again. It is true that you can fool some of the people some of the time, but usually only once. If it is your aim to use media advertising to build lists for direct mail, don't sacrifice goodwill by creating disappointment and mistrust right from the first sale.

It is normal in advertising copy for generalized, emotive language to be used, but in off-the-page direct response advertising the wording has to consist of precise word pictures. It is another kind of copywriting altogether, and that is where a specialist direct marketing advertising agency should score, and not only in artwork and media buying.

You can sell all kinds of things off-the-page. They include foreign stamps, collectibles such as coins, unit trusts, insurance, clothes, books, jewellery, furniture, tableware, holidays, horticultural products, shares, savings, charity appeals, language courses and records, to name but a few.

The John Harvey Collection promotes 30 products a year, mostly fashion and footwear lines, and has continued to prosper with off-the-page advertising since first offering and selling 24 000 pendant watches in 1978. They also have a customer mailing list of 700 000 which is mailed twice a year with leaflets. About £1.8m a year is spent on press advertising, and the same small agency has been used for several years. Most of their lines are British made, and good purchasing plus consistent advertising have made this firm succeed when so many of those which featured in the colour supplements in the 1970s and 1980s have disappeared.

According to a Gallup survey, 60 per cent of people take their information from the press. Print media remains predominant, whether for news or advertising. Television has not destroyed the press, any more than the gramophone or tape recorder destroyed the playing of instruments. The press has even increased in number of titles as a result of TV, which has created new topics to be written and read about. There are, for instance, more than 260 British computer magazines, and all told there are more than 12 000 British publications.

Whether or not you use an advertising agency, it is essential to consider the elements in the next section.

ELEMENTS OF OFF-THE-PAGE ADVERTISING

Media

The budget, and its allocation to various media resulting in a planned media schedule of insertions, needs to be prepared at least six months in advance. Actual choice of merchandise and production of creative work may be decided at shorter intervals, dependent on copy dates, with lead times depending on the kind of publication. Advertisement rates need to be judged not just by the rate card but by the cost per thousand readers or circulation and by the demographic characteristics of the readers. Success can also depend on date, position and size of insertions – as well as on imponderables such as the weather and political/economic situations. A very small advertisement can succeed if it is accompanied by similar ads in a sort of market-place on your subject, such as holiday ads.

The economics of advertising are based on cost per thousand readers or circulation. Readership is estimated by JICNARS who conduct surveys, while circulation is the ABC figure based on average audited net sales per issue. Readership can be three or more times the circulation figure. The circulation of the *Financial Times* is small compared with that of the *Sun*, but more people read one copy of the *FT* than do the *Sun*. Magazines often found in waiting rooms usually have a high secondary readership, such as *Reader's Digest*. Free newspapers usually have larger circulations than paid-for local newspapers, because of their house-by-house penetration. You cannot therefore judge by rate alone.

You also have to compare both response and conversion into sales. If you key your advertisements (by printing a date or number on the coupon, such as DM1, DM2 for succeeding insertions in the *Daily Mail*), you can count the replies to each advertisement. If you divide the number of replies into the cost of the space you will arrive at a cost per reply. Each insertion will produce a different result, not just for each publication but for each date and each different product. Thus you can discover the most economic medium, the best days or dates, and the most attractive product. You may have to add some value judgements about circumstances which influenced those results.

Cost per conversion can be even more interesting. The insertion which produces the most replies may not necessarily produce the most or the best conversions if your ad is aimed at getting catalogue requests, and vice versa. Keying is discussed more fully in Chapter 16 on research.

By these analyses you (and your agency if you use one) can arrive at the most economical media list for future campaigns. It is quite remarkable how seemingly similar newspapers or magazines will produce contrary results. The trick is to spend the least to get the most. You will find that this sort of careful research may reveal that it pays to advertise in certain media only on particular dates, and you have to be insistent about this, whatever hard-selling advertisement salesmen or even your agency say.

Design

This is where your agency can help, especially if you need to illustrate goods, perhaps in colour. Your advertisement is your shop window and you are a retailer. The advertisement needs to be properly dressed so that your merchandise is presented as attractively, authentically and realistically as possible. The reader must be able to see exactly what he or she is being persuaded to buy. At this point you may care to reread Chapter 12 on photography.

Laying out the pictures and wording requires creative skill if the advertisement is to attract attention, arouse interest, create desire, inspire confidence and provoke action. Remember, an advertisement has to compete for attention, and although print is static it has to stimulate eye movement through the words and pictures to the point of filling in a coupon and mailing it.

Copy

The wording must be appropriate to the medium and the reader. What may suit the *News of the World* may not suit the *Sunday Telegraph*. You may have a lot to say, but make sure that it is not only informative and persuasive but readable and legible and that it is set out so that the reader is induced to read it.

Short words, short sentences and short paragraphs, use of white space for clarity or emphasis, and avoidance of unfamiliar words all help to get your copy read. If a reader stops at a word they do not know or understand, the reading flow is halted and you have lost them. Nowadays, people do not read; they skip and skim. You may have to keep them reading by using devices like subheadings and italic or bold type. These typographical effects have to be thought of when the copy is being written.

Coupons

The writing of coupons is an art in itself. Make sure, too, that your name and address is printed in the advertisement as well as on the coupon, in case people want it after they have cut the coupon. The point is often overlooked.

What do you want your customer to tell you? Full name, address, telephone number, position, sex, age? If a *choice* is to be made, make sure it is easy to state on the coupon or order form, perhaps with boxes to tick. Alternative choices may be important, so that you can supply without further correspondence if you are out of stock of the first choice. Is there enough *space* for the customer to give you the information you need? Is the coupon well *positioned* so that it is easy to clip? Dot lines and even scissor signs can help to get the coupon cut out.

Coupons are essential in off-the-page ads – unless you want to deter frivolous replies, when it may be preferable to use a telephone number – but even so, will readers take the trouble to clip the coupon? Will they wish to damage a favourite magazine which they like to keep? When, for instance, will they cut one on a programme page of the *Radio Times* or *TV Times*: at the end of its ten-day life, if they remember?

What about positioning? Coupons have been known to

back each other! One device which can resolve these problems, especially inertia, is the pull-off reply card (with business reply or Freepost facility). Such cards are novel, invite response, need no envelope, and are easily and quickly returned. Kitchens Direct, in weekend colour magazines, have even repeated the coupon below the peel-off postcard.

As already mentioned, coupons can be keyed so that response can be identified for source, counted and evaluated. Keys can be introduced into addresses by a change of initial if a personal name is used, or by including a room or department number. However, this can depend on people writing the address correctly. A simple method is to print a distinctive key on the coupon, using a different one for each insertion.

AUDIO AND VIDEO TAPES

These are devices which take your spoken or visual message right into the home or office. An audio tape can also be played back in the car. Audio tapes have been offered by Gartmore and videos by Kleinwort Benson to promote unit trusts. Holiday firms offer the loan of videos, while the Cyprus Tourist Board has advertised audio tapes – rather appropriately in radio commercials.

INSERTS

The attractions of inserts are that they allow you to say more than in an advertisement space, and they cost less than advertisement space. They are widely used in magazines. One direct response agency handles 200 million inserts a year. But a large print run is necessary, and there can be a high wastage factor.

Like junk mail, inserts can be resented, and some readers automatically tip inserts into the bin before reading the journal. Inserts can therefore be a nuisance. And yet one finds the same advertisers repeatedly using inserts, and claiming that they save postage. They piggyback on to the large circulations of journals which penetrate the right market. There are a lot of pros and cons!

Sound advice

FREE FRONTIER MARKETS TRUST CASSETTE OFFER

Since Gartmore launched the Frontier Markets Trust in February this year its value has grown 38%* and has attracted over £50 million of investors' money.

In the judgement of the Trust's Managers it still has a long way to go.

If you telephone the Investor Services Department **FREE** on *0800-289 336* or simply fill in the coupon, we will send you a copy of a specially produced tape cassette which tells you more about this remarkable Trust.

And how to be part of its future.

To: Gartmore Fund Managers Ltd., Frontier Markets Cassette Offer, Gartmore House, 16-18 Monument Street, London EC3R 8AJ.

Please send my free copy of the tape and brochure.

BLOCK CAPITALS PLEASE

Name
(Mr/Mrs/Miss/Title)_____

Address_____

_____

_____

_____

Postcode_____ 0279

Gartmore

*Source: IDC/Opal 24th September 1987 offer to bid net income reinvested.

An example of an audio tape offer to promote unit trusts. The coupon bears a key.

So let us think about the characteristics of inserts, their strengths and weaknesses, special applications and ways of making them work.

Survival   Not only are inserts likely to be discarded; their life is not likely to survive beyond the original reader, whereas an advertisement printed in the journal will continue working as long as the copy of the journal lives. There can be short-term response from an insert compared with long-term response from a space advertisement. On the other hand, if the first reader is sufficiently interested to extract the insert he will mail in the coupon or at least keep the insert for further reference.

Size of insert   The size and shape of an insert may effect interest in it. If it is similar in format to the page of the journal in which it is inserted, it may be retained because it seems to be part of the issue, like the single slip sheets in newspapers. If it is of smaller size or different in shape it is obviously something tipped in and separate from the journal.

Hit-or-miss effect   Perhaps it is a delusion that inserts are a waste of money because so many people do tip them in the bin. If only the occasional reader takes an interest and responds, that is good business. Do all the thousands of readers of newspapers and magazines read every advertisement? More selective though it may be, does direct mail have large percentage response? It can be quite economic to mail 5000 shots to get 50 orders, if their value is substantial. It all depends what it costs to make a sale. That cost may still be a tiny fraction of the selling price.

They are unavoidable   Inserts thrust themselves upon readers. You might say they fall into readers' hands. They are intrusive, begging for attention, whether discarded or not. They score in this respect over the fixed, more static space advertisement.

Editions or circulations can be selective   Especially with controlled circulation journals, it is possible to limit insertions to copies sent to particular groups of readers. Except with regional or international editions, it is not possible to limit advertisements to certain readers. This restricted use of inserts can be used to test response. In the case of some journals it is possible to target inserts by ACORN area or even town distribution.

In lieu of a good mailing list   Very often, inserts are used for lack of something better and because the cost of space advertising is prohibitive. Usually, this means lack of a good mailing list. In other words, inserts can be a poor alternative to direct mail.

Some of today's inserts are more than leaflets. One type is the sealed plain envelope – but does it cause sufficient curiosity to get it opened, or is it one of the more easily binned items? Many gift catalogues are now inserted, but there are so many gift and novelty catalogues that saturation can bore. They come through the mail, or as mail drops, and more recently as inserts; there is surely a limit to what people will buy. There are times when direct response marketing seems to suffer from overkill.

15   Mail drops

Door-to-door distribution of leaflets is one of the oldest forms of advertising, and has long been a favourite medium of local shopkeepers and tradesmen. With specialist distributors, the use of ACORN targeting, and the ready-made distribution networks of the free newspapers, mail dropping has become more sophisticated. Multiple mail drops have become commonplace.

Householders may well wonder what next is coming through the letterbox or is to be left in the porch. They may not always appreciate the littered mat when several items are delivered together. To return from holiday is to walk through a sea of scattered paper!

It is a cheap but not always cheerful medium, the print often being crude. The question is: what will the housewife value? She is flooded with photo processors' envelopes, cards from window cleaners and car hire operators, premium vouchers, offers of double glazing and window replacements, appeals for property from estate agents, and assorted free magazines and catalogues. You name it, she gets it. More for the bin! There ought to be a clutter code.

And yet it can be an effective medium if used judiciously. The trouble is it suffers too often from indiscriminate saturation distribution.

One of the all time greats of doorstoppers was surely the one which used to arrive as advance publicity for the circus when I was a small boy. A children's colouring card picturing a circus scene was delivered house to house. If you coloured the card and took it to the box office you got a free ticket, but, of course, you had to be accompanied by an adult who had to buy a ticket!

The secret of success with this medium is that the shot needs to be enlivened by some ingenuity, and to be of interest and value to the recipient. That is not easy if it is even more static and mundane than, say, a direct mail shot, which at least requires the effort of opening it.

Perhaps it pays to enclose the mail drop in some way – but is the answer an unaddressed sealed plain envelope? The housewife may be coaxed into opening it, thinking maybe that it is a greetings card from a neighbour or a note from a friend. The result can be an anticlimax. This device has been used by the Cheltenham and Gloucester Building Society to announce the opening of a new branch.

The plain envelope ploy is also used by estate agents seeking property to sell. There is another danger apart from the commercial let-down when the contents were expected to be more personal. The unaddressed envelope also implies that the sender does not know the person's identity or, worse still, could not be bothered to address it personally. There are some perils here. The recipient's likely reaction should be gauged carefully.

RESEARCH

Circular Distributors (CD), said to be the largest UK door-to-door distributors with a £10m annual turnover, conducted a survey in 1987 in an attempt to find out how to improve the bad reputation of and gain credibility for doorstoppers. The survey was conducted by Millward Brown (MB). The results were published in an article by David Gerie in *Marketing* (July 16, 1987). The following summary is encouraging, but it also highlights certain findings which are worth discussing.

Two matched samples of housewives were selected for distribution and later for questioning. The first was a control group of 200 who all received a shared mailing and were visited by MB interviewers, and the second was a test group of 400 to whom CD distributed items. The mail drops were from an electrical and photographic retailer, a fast food chain, a detergent manufacturer, a mail order firm, a soup manufacturer and others. The main findings were:

1 14 per cent of housewives said they never looked at the material.

2 57 per cent said they usually looked at and read items of interest.

3 Working housewives as well as non-working housewives, whether middle or working class, expressed this interest.

4 Northern housewives (61 per cent) were slightly more likely than those of the south to read items of interest.

5 39 per cent liked receiving letterbox drops, others being neutral rather than hostile.

6 Younger housewives (under 34) were 'particularly appreciative' of door-to-door distribution.

7 Working housewives were more interested in such items than those who did not go out to work.

8 Some 70 per cent of the total sample, with similar age, class and working/non-working differences applying, liked free samples.

9 85 per cent of the test sample claimed to have received at least one of the items, compared with 89 per cent in the control group.

10 The electrical retailer, whose leaflet was the largest, was remembered by 83 per cent of the control group, but percentages fell to 52 and 50 for the packet soup and one of the detergents, and were even lower for the mail order items.

11 43 per cent of those recalling the detergent leaflets were pleased with them, but the score was only 13 per cent for approval of the leaflet from the electrical and photographic retailer, perhaps because its appeal was to men. The fast food chain item pleased only 17 per cent. Only 2 per cent approved the mail order material; in fact, it annoyed 20 per cent.

12 More than 25 per cent had redeemed their detergent coupons, but many had thrown them away.

The report is available free of charge from Millward Brown Market Research Ltd, Ince House, 60 Kenilworth Road, Leamington Spa, Warwickshire CV32 6JY.

From these findings can be pulled out some significant facts.

Younger housewives seem to be the least resistant; items have to be of interest; free samples are liked; and money-off vouchers produce a good response. Perhaps working housewives were more interested because they had more personal spending money as distinct from housekeeping money. Presumably the researched items were well produced and superior to other items received, but nevertheless the wastage factor was still high. Against this has to be reckoned that mail drops are cheaper than press advertisements, the distribution cost being £20 per 1000 unshared items in addition to print costs. According to Nick Wells of Circular Distributors, the redemption rate for coupons distributed door-to-door can be about 10.1 per cent compared with 1–4 per cent with press advertising.

TARGETING AND DISTRIBUTION

The quality of the mail drop and its interest and value to the recipient, calls for ingenuity and creative skills. However, the medium is not favoured by advertising agencies, and lack of creativity may be one of the bogies, resulting in tatty leaflets. On the other hand, in-house direct response marketing departments (especially of financial firms) are exploiting door-to-door distribution.

The cost aspect can be a temptation. A mail drop costs about a tenth of a direct mail shot, which usually contains more print, an envelope and a reply envelope, and requires postage. One of the most economical ways to distribute is together with a free newspaper (not as an insert), and that can be 50 per cent cheaper than using a specialist door-to-door distributor who has to employ teams of distributors.

Again, by targeting with ACORN much wasteful distribution can be eliminated. Target Distribution of Chingford, for instance, have joined with CACI (creators of ACORN) to produce a postcode sector boundary map for selective locational distribution. They can reach 17 million out of a possible 20 million households.

Another distributor, Network Letterbox Marketing of London, operates a Matchmaker system of household targeting on a socio-economic neighbourhood basis. Areas can be chosen by TV region, city or town, postal sector or demographic profile, with solus or shared drops. This is linked to free newspaper distribution. Nationwide coverage of 18.5 million homes can be reached in three days, every week. Each distributor averages 250 deliveries, and there are 80 000 back checks every week.

In the UK there are some 40 national or regional door-to-door distributors, not forgetting Royal Mail Household Deliveries which uses postmen to average three items per drop. This service also offers targeting facilities. Profiles can be selected by town, county, region, postcode district and sector or TV area. Deliveries are over an agreed two-week delivery period, and items have to be supplied a week in advance to each of the Head Post Offices involved. This does mean that deliveries will not be as prompt or as simultaneous as distribution with free newspapers, when the whole distribution can be completed in three days.

Shareplans
A number of door-to-door distributors offer monthly shareplan services whereby several non-conflicting items are dropped at the same time. Opinions differ as to whether this attracts more attention than a single drop, or whether the litter effect is more irritating than a single drop. But as always, so much depends on the merits of the items.

Shopping Magazines
These are omnibus volumes of coupon offers by different firms. It is a bumper money-off offer, and recipients are encouraged to look through and select the vouchers most useful to them. These shopping magazines lend themselves particularly to lines easily purchased at supermarkets.

*   *   *

Mail drops need to be considered very carefully. They may be very useful for zonal campaigns aimed at enlivening low-selling areas, or to support local branches. A mail drop campaign can be executed fairly quickly, and may be useful for an urgent sales drive.

16 How to research and record results

Some aspects of research have already been touched on in previous chapters, with an interesting study being outlined in Chapter 15. Keying and calculating cost per reply and cost per conversion were discussed in Chapter 14, and will be elaborated on in this chapter.

KEYING

To arrive at the efficiency of any medium it is necessary to *identify* the source of response. This may seem to be easy if response is thought to be coming from an annual or a seasonal catalogue, but this is not necessarily so. It is surprising how often people keep old material and order from it months or years later. You may recognize the order form, but they may write a letter or phone you. Your only clue may be that the price has changed or you no longer stock the merchandise. Some magazines have remarkably long lives, and customers may send you orders in response to old off-the-page advertisements. Identification of source becomes even more important if you advertise frequently.

Identification can be achieved in a variety of simple ways. You may not want the customer to be involved or perhaps even be aware that you are conducting a check. It is possible to have distorted returns if the customer spots your keying device in two advertisements and decides to use the key in what is thought to be the most important medium. This has been noted when the same advertisement has appeared in a national and a regional newspaper, and customers returned the coupon in the national newspaper although both had been seen. The repetition may, of course, have been useful in reinforcing interest.

Here are some methods of keying, and you must decide which is the most appropriate in your case:

1 If a real or imaginary name is included in the address, it can be varied for each medium or insertion. People are generally careful to give the correct address when they want something. Reply envelopes can be sorted according to key, and attributed to each source. For a campaign consisting of advertisements in numerous newspapers I once used my own name in the address but the initial ranged from A to Z, which made identification very easy.

2 If you want to know the areas of the country from which replies come, you can retain and sort envelopes into towns. This can reveal the volume of response from different towns. With this information you can decide on which areas to concentrate future effort, which to eliminate or maybe which need stronger effort. Reply envelopes can be a rich source of ready-made in-house research.

3 Keys can be printed discreetly on coupons, showing which insertion, in which publication and on which date, produced the response.

4 Serial numbers can be printed on all kinds of print such as prize coupons and order forms, and you can determine which series of numbers – perhaps with prefixes – is used each time.

5 Different coloured return items can be used in succeeding mailings. You can use a different colour for ink or paper. Colour coding can be applied to reply envelopes or cards, coupons or order forms. This can be very useful with piggybacked mailings. If, for example, you were piggy-backing on gas and electricity bills you could use one colour insert for gas and one for electricity.

6 Different typography is another way of identifying response. One item may be printed in sanserif type and another in serif type, and the distinction will identify response.

When your incoming mail is researched in these ways you can

make your promotional effort more efficient. It can produce the following information:

1   Which publications should be used for future advertising.
2   Which dates or days of the week produce the best and which the worst response.
3   Where geographically the response comes from.
4   The cost per enquiry or order, or the cost per conversion from enquiries to orders.

You can go further and analyse the responses themselves, and especially orders. If you use a personal computer to record enquiries and orders you can apply appropriate searches. Thus you can discover the following about the respondents:

Male or female
Age
Position
Location
Item(s) purchased
Value of order(s)
Repeat buyers
Non-repeat buyers

This information can help in producing future media schedules; maintaining databases and mailing lists; the use of geodemographic targeting (such as ACORN); and the choice of merchandise.

MEDIA AND COPY TESTING

You may plan to undertake off-the-page advertising: but in which publications will you advertise? You can compare rates on publishers' rate cards or in *British Rate and Data*, and study ABC circulation figures and JICNARS readership figures and demographic profiles. Your advertising agency can put all the data into a computer and come up with a model media schedule.

But there is still no certainty that the *Daily Porn* will be more effective and economic than the *Daily Image*. One way to be more positive is to have split runs or to use regional editions of national publications. A very interesting brochure on this is published by Direct Response Media Ltd of Richmond, Surrey. Two methods combine media and copy testing:

A/B split method This entails printing a control and a test advertisement in different copies of the same publication, on the same day and in the same position, and comparing the response from each. Similarly, you can do this with different radio and TV stations or, better still, different transmitters from the same TV station.

Crossover test Run different ads in different journals and then switch the ads for two more issues of these two journals.

Copy testing can also be conducted by traditional street or doorstep interviews, when a sample of prospects is asked to study and recall parts of a series of proposed advertisements. Different research firms have their particular techniques. These range from the folder method, in which different advertisements are displayed one by one by the interviewer, to the reading and noting and recall tests, when respondents are asked what they remember of an advertisement which appeared the previous day. These and other types of copy testing can help to eliminate bad points or enhance or vary others in the layout or copy. However, if willingness to buy is registered you do have to allow for the fact that the advertisement was seen in isolation, and that when the advertisement eventually appears willingness to buy may not necessarily be translated into actual purchase.

Nevertheless, these kinds of research can be valuable in perfecting advertisements and avoiding mistakes. The creators of advertisements may be very clever, but tested reactions may produce surprising results. The creators may think they are right, or you may choose what you think is the best copy and presentation, but you could all be wrong. Some prize-winning advertising campaigns have been failures in the marketplace. You can be too clever sometimes.

Ten Golden Rules of Testing
In their brochure, Direct Response Media offer the following sage advice:

1　Remember, test results do not necessarily transmute between companies, products, media, seasons and so on.
2　Test the big issues first, that is those whose outcome is likely to have greatest bearing on your objectives.
3　Never believe a single test result: repeat important tests at least three times or more if the spaces are small or the response low.
4　Never forget a test result. Keep a 'bible' of results and refer to it often.
5　Test market variables in preference to style of copy, that is test product, price, proposition and premium before words, pictures and layout.
6　Keep an eye out for other people's tests and try to piece together their conclusions.
7　Never forget a test opportunity: there is always a question someone in your organization would like to have answered.
8　Progress advertisement by advertisement and not campaign by campaign, allowing yourself to be influenced by test results as they become conclusive.
9　Remember: inexpensive tests are often the most fruitful.
10　Do not let testing atrophy your judgement: you will need judgement to know what to test.

COLOUR TESTING

You may have your favourite colour or colours, but do your customers share your preferences? Do they react favourably or unfavourably to your colours? Comment has been made elsewhere in this book on the muddle of items contained in a mail shot. There can also be a muddle of conflicting colours.

There is a language and a psychology of colour. This is very true if you are exporting. In some countries black is for mourning, in other countries it is white. To Asiatics, pale blue is a sad colour. Muslims tend to like green, while Chinese love red and gold.

Some colours like red and orange come forward, while pastel shades like mauve recede. Young people, and especially children, like red. Yellow tends to reflect hope and happiness, while green can appeal to go-getters.

There are obviously some generalizations here, but you may find it useful to include colour in your researches, and test what response you get to the use of different colours. Which colour is best if you want to be conservative, abrasive or the bringer of good news? Which are the best seasonal colours: perhaps yellow in the spring, blue in the summer, brown in the autumn and red in the winter?

TESTING PRICE

The price you charge may affect your sales, but which is the price which will produce the most sales? Some goods may sell because they are bargains or because a high price gives status. A British firm, making excellent British-made watches, failed to sell their watches because they were too cheap. People often judge quality by price. There is also a market price which people expect to pay for certain goods. Don't be afraid of price: it is surprising what people will pay if they think the price is right. Sometimes price has to do with satisfaction; people enjoy something because it cost so much. Is a Rolls-Royce worth four times the price of an average good car? If you own one you will be certain the price was right. But if you don't?

In direct response marketing it is possible to test price by conducting sample mailings of the same product at different prices to find out which one pulls the most sales. The variation in price may be slight, and you alone cannot always assess the right price. It is not just a matter of adding a percentage to costs. A few pence up or down may make all the difference.

OFFER TESTING

This involves testing either the merchandise or the pro-position. Once again samples of the prospect list can be tested or, as discussed earlier, split run and regional editions can be used to test alternative products.

Getting the offer right is essential, and this was discussed at the beginning of this book as one of the basic secrets of successful direct response marketing. But how far do you rely on your buying and promotional skills, and how often do you actually put products to the test before going a bundle on them? This also includes free gifts and other devices to stimulate action.

Are the frills really necessary? Cannot the merchandise sell on its merits? Does a gift invite doubt about the offer? It's worth testing these alternatives – the straight proposition and the addition of some gimmick or freebie.

In testing, two rules have to be obeyed. First, the sample must be large enough to be representative of typical customers. Second, if you normally sell nationally, the test including the medium used must be a miniature of the broad-scale market.

FINANCIAL DIRECT MARKETING

This is probably the largest field of direct marketing; it embraces insurance companies, banks, unit trusts, building societies, brokers and other financial institutions. Of special interest to such direct marketers is the *Nationwide Market Research Report* published by Nationwide Market Research Ltd of Camberley, Surrey. This survey on life insurance analyses the industry's effort and investment over the first six months of 1987.

The report is based on a review of 65 000 advertisements from numerous publications across a network of 13 TV regions. In a grid format it presents data on advertising share statistics, media utilization, response devices and incentives presented. Facts are given on use of colour, payment devices, closing dates and limited editions, and there is a case history on Sun Alliance's black and white advertisements versus Royal Heritage's use of inserts.

If you are interested in how other financial direct marketers do it, an investment of £295 plus VAT in a copy may be worth while.

17   Voluntary and legal controls

The advertising industry is subject to more than 100 statutes and regulations, and a number of codes of practice. The direct response marketer needs to be aware of these controls, and to keep up to date with new laws as they are promulgated.

In this chapter there will be an introduction to the voluntary controls, but copies of these codes should be obtained from the authorities which administer them. There is also an introduction to some of the more recent and relevant legislation, plus the MOPS scheme operated by the national newspapers. The subject is vast: several books have been written on advertising law, but it has been prohibitive to keep them up to date and they have each gone out of print. Copies of statutes and regulations can be purchased from HM Stationery Offices.

BRITISH CODE OF ADVERTISING PRACTICE

This code is administered by the Advertising Standards Association, and is published by the Code of Advertising Practice Committee, Brook House, 2–16 Torrington Place, London WC1E 7HN (telephone 01 580 5555).

Members of the public are invited to send written complaints to the ASA at this address. Every month its findings are published in the monthly *ASA Reports*, copies of which are supplied free on request. These findings are frequently quoted in the press, so whether a complaint is upheld or not it is widely publicized. It does not pay to incur criticism! The code has been in force since 1962, the seventh edition being published in October 1985.

The ASA has published frequent warnings about off-the-

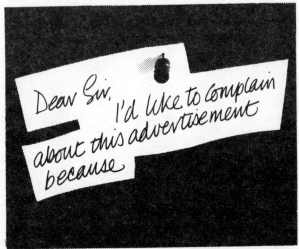

Most advertisements are legal, decent, honest and truthful. A few are not, and, like you, we want them stopped.

If you would like to know more about how to make complaints, please send for our booklet: 'The Do's and Don'ts of Complaining'. It's free.

The Advertising Standards Authority.

We're here to put it right. ✓

ASA Ltd., Dept. Z, Brook House, Torrington Place, London WC1E 7HN.

This space is donated in the interests of high standards of advertising.

page offers by inexperienced direct response firms and especially individuals such as those offering computer software. Sometimes newcomers to direct response do not appreciate the power of advertising; they become swamped by enquiries or orders which they cannot handle quickly, and complaints are provoked by the delay.

The ASA has four subcommittees to which investigations are remitted, and one of them deals specifically with mail order and direct response advertising.

Section C. VI sets out eleven sections of recommendations regarding mail order and direct response advertising, and also draws attention to legislation such as the Consumer Safety Act 1978, the Hallmarking Act 1973, the Post Office Act 1953, the Mail Order Transactions (Information) Order 1976, and the European Communities Act 1972.

In particular, the BCAP refers to conformity of goods to relevant standards; conformity of goods to description; goods sent on approval; the advertiser's address; mailing and packaging; cash with order; fulfilment of the order; and media requirements. Very important is the identification of the advertiser.

Offences against BCAP are committed by large and small direct response marketers, mostly unintentionally, but also by others who are quite cynical about their abuse of advertising. *A very common cause of complaint is delay in delivery*; the ASA receives 30–40 such complaints a month!

Here are some typical cases reported in the *ASA* Case Report 154 (February 1988): the references are to parts of BCAP.

Basis of complaint A member of the public objected to a specialist press mail order advertisement for computer software which appeared in May 1987. The complainant ordered one of the software items, entitled Tube. However, he received a reply stating that the title would not be available until July. He was later informed that it would be further delayed until September. He therefore questioned the advertising on an item which was not available. (Parts B.14; C. VI.10; C. VI.11.2)

Conclusion Complaint upheld. The advertisers stated that the advertisement was simply intended to make the reader aware of a forthcoming product and was not intended to be a mail order advertisement with a coupon for direct response. The Authority noted this but considered that the advertisement for a product which is not yet available should make clear the intended date of release of the product. The advertisers were requested to include such a reference in future advertisements of this nature.

Basis of complaint   A member of the public objected to a direct mail leaflet which featured a telephone answering machine on the cover in conjunction with the statement 'from only £99.00'. The inside of the catalogue described the machine at £99.00 as the KX-T24 16 DBE. The complainant contacted the advertisers to purchase the unit but was informed that it cost £189.00. He therefore questioned the price quoted in the leaflet. (Parts B.5.1; B.7.3.2)

Conclusion   Complaint upheld. The advertisers stated that, owing to a proof-reading error, the leaflet was printed with the incorrect prices and this was not noticed until the leaflets had been distributed. They further stated that the cover, which included the statement 'Telephone answering machines from only £99.00' in conjunction with a picture of a machine, simply indicated that answering machines were available at a price of £99.00 and not that the pictured machine was available at that price. The Authority nonetheless believed that the approach was open to misconstruction and reminded the advertisers that, when products are illustrated in conjunction with a price, the code requires advertisers to ensure that the illustrated item can be purchased for the price shown.

Basis of complaint   A member of the public objected to a mail order catalogue which included the claim that a clothes press, the Singer Press 111, was approved to BSI standards. The complainant understood that the product had not passed BSI standards and therefore questioned the inclusion of the claim. (Part B.5.1)

Conclusion   Complaint upheld. The advertisers supplied a certificate of compliance showing that the product had been tested to relevant safety regulations. The Authority noted that they did not consider this to be sufficient basis for the claims, which the advertisers were requested to amend to reflect the nature of the testing carried out.

BRITISH CODE OF SALES PROMOTION PRACTICE

Also administered by the Advertising Standards Authority,

this is concerned with 'premium offers of all kinds; reduced price and free offers; the distribution of vouchers, coupons and samples; personality promotions; charity-linked promotions; and prize promotions of all types'.

Many of these marketing techniques may be applied to direct response marketing, whatever media may be used. The code also lists 19 legislative controls ranging from the Consumer Credit Act 1974 to the Unsolicited Goods and Services Act 1971.

Section 6 says: 'Particular care should be taken to avoid misuse of the word "gift".' Also under Section 6 are guidelines relating to free offers: 'It is not legitimate for promotions to recoup the cost to them of a free offer: by imposing charges they would not normally make; by inflating beyond their actual level any expenses they incur on postage, freight, etc.; by altering the composition or quality, or by increasing the price, of any product which must be bought in order to qualify for the offer.'

There is also a section on mailing lists – their accuracy, confidentiality, and responsibility for removing names if requested. Reference is made to the Mailing Preference Service.

BRITISH DIRECT MARKETING ASSOCIATION CODE OF PRACTICE AND TELEPHONE MARKETING GUIDELINES

Grosvenor Gardens House, Grosvenor Gardens, London SW1W 0BS (telephone: 01 630 7322)

The BDMA code was first published on November 1, 1981 and became effective on January 1, 1982. It aimed to govern the conduct of its members, who included direct mail advertisers, direct response mail order companies and other direct response advertisers. In accepting the code, members of the Association accept an obligation to the public. In recognition of that obligation they adopt methods of trading which are wholly consistent with the public interest and the highest standards of fair trading. Breaches of the code are subject to the disciplinary provisions of the memorandum and articles of the Association.

The BDMA Code of Practice supplements and complements the British Code of Advertising Practice and the British Code of Sales Promotion Practice. Certain sections of the BCAP are repeated in original or amended form where appropriate. However, such use and/or amendment does not detract from the commitment to the full BCAP which is accepted by all members of the BDMA.

Member companies of the BDMA identify themselves as members of the BDMA in their advertisements and literature, and the Association publicizes the concilation and arbitration services available to the public through its code.

It is therefore very much to the advantage of a direct response marketing company to be seen to be a member of the BDMA.

A number of changes have taken place in the industry, other codes and in new legislation, and the BDMA Code of Practice was substantially revised in 1988.

Telephone Marketing Guidelines

As mentioned in Chapter 13, the BDMA has drawn up guidelines for telephone marketing. These are reproduced here as they are important to anyone involved in selling by telephone. These guidelines are also reassuring to members of the public in that they show that the organized industry does take its responsibilities seriously.

Introduction

The British Direct Marketing Association Guidelines for Telephone Marketing Practices are intended to provide organizations involved in direct telephone marketing to both consumers and businesses with principles of ethical and professional conduct.

All members of the BDMA shall comply with any relevant legislation which may supersede these guidelines. In addition, all members shall comply with the following guidelines in respect of activities not covered by specific law, or when legal requirements are less restrictive than the guidelines.

Disclosure

1 The name of the company on whose behalf a sales and marketing call is made or received should be voluntarily and promptly disclosed, and this information repeated on request at any time during the conversation.

2 The purpose of the call should be made clear at the start, and the content of the call should be restricted to matters directly relevant to its purpose.

3 The name, address and telephone number of the company responsible for the call should appear in the telephone directory, or be available through directory enquiries, or be readily available through another source. This information shall also be given on request.

4 If a telephone marketer is acting as an agent of a company, the name, address and telephone number of the agent should be disclosed upon request at any time during the conversation.

5 If a person phoned was recommended by a third party, the identity of the third party should be voluntarily and promptly disclosed.

Honesty

1 Telephone marketers should not evade the truth or deliberately mislead. Any questions should be answered honestly and fully to the best of the knowledge available.

2 Sales and marketing calls should not be executed in the guise of research or a survey. In cases where the words 'research' or 'survey' are used the information obtained must not be used to form the basis of a direct sales approach either during or after the call.

3 Companies should accept responsibility for statements made by their sales staff or agents.

Reasonable hours

1 Telephone marketers should avoid making sales and marketing calls during hours which are unreasonable to the recipients of the calls, bearing in mind that the OFT recommends that calls to consumers should not be made later than 9.00 p.m. unless expressly invited and that what

is regarded as unreasonable can vary in different parts of the country and in different types of households or businesses.

2   When sales and marketing calls are initiated by a company or its representatives, telephone marketers should ask whether the timing of a call is convenient. If it is not, they should offer to ring back at a more convenient time.

Courtesy and procedures

1   Normal rules of telephone courtesy should be observed. Telephone marketers should avoid the use of high-pressure tactics which could be construed as harassment.
2   Telephone marketers should always recognize the right of the other party to terminate the telephone conversation at any stage, and should accept such termination promptly and courteously.
3   If, as a result of a telephone contact, an appointment is made whereby a representative of a company is to visit a consumer at home, the consumer should be provided with a clearly identified contact point in order to facilitate possible cancellation or alteration of the appointment.
4   Confirmation of any order placed should be sent to the customer and any documents forwarded in accordance with the prevailing legislation.
5   Telephone marketers should take particular care not to seek information or to accept orders or appointments or invite any other action from a minor.
6   When consumer sales and marketing calls are made by a company or its representatives, there should be a cooling-off period of at least 7 days for oral contracts resulting from such calls, and the recipients of the calls should be so informed.

Restriction of contacts

1   Sales and marketing calls should not be generated by random or sequential dialling manually or by computer.
2   Sales and marketing calls should not knowingly be made to unlisted or ex-directory numbers.
3   Unless expressly invited consumer calls should not be made to individuals at their place of work.

4 Members should subscribe to the Telephone Preference Service (when it becomes available).
5 Members should delete from their telephone contact lists those persons who have specifically requested not to be contacted by telephone for sales or marketing purposes.
6 When sales and marketing calls are initiated by a company or its representatives and automatic message and recording equipment is used, it is necessary either to:
(a) Immediately effect an introduction on the lines of 'This is a computer call on behalf of . . .'; or
(b) Have a 'live' operator introduce the call under those circumstances where the nature of the call is of a personal or a sensitive nature.

Definitions
1 *Business calling* Sales and marketing calls for an individual as a representative of his or her company.
2 *Consumer calling* Sales and marketing calls for an individual not as a representative of his or her employer or company.
3 *Sales and marketing call* A call designed to generate a sale of a product or service, or to lead towards a sale of a product or service, to the specific company or consumer as a result of the information given during a telephone conversation.

BRITISH LIST BROKERS ASSOCIATION TRADING PRACTICE GUIDE

Premier House, 150 Southampton Row, London WC1B 5AL (telephone: 01 278 0236)

This Trading Practice Guide has been drawn up by the List Brokers Association to assist in the practices and conduct of full and associate members of BLBA in their dealings with each other, list owners and users.

The British List Brokers Association is committed to support the broad aims of the British Direct Marketing Association and Direct Mail Producers Association. Much of the Trading Practice Guide is complementary to the codes of practice as adhered to by the members of BDMA and DMPA and British Code of Advertising Practice.

All members of the BLBA are strongly urged to apply the guide in practice and spirit; its application will be self-regulatory.

In the event of complaints made against any member of the Association, the General Management Committee will use the guide in respect of the alleged dispute (refer to complaints procedure for details).

The overriding value of the guide is the promotion of greater harmony and understanding of working methods of members, list owners and users. The guide sets out the rights, responsibilities and liabilities of list owners, list managers and list brokers, and the procedure regarding complaints and disputes.

CONSUMER PROTECTION ACT 1987

The most far-reaching of all consumer protection legislation, this Act contains many changes in the law of which the direct response marketer must be aware.

It deals with product liability, consumer safety and mis-leading prices. It imposes liability for unlimited damages on producers, importers and own labellers for defects which cause injury or death without proof of either negligence or contractual relationship. This calls for a general duty to sell safe products, and this duty is additional to existing safety legislation. All previous law on price indications is replaced by the Act, which seeks to impose tougher controls of bogus price offers.

In effect it means that mail order traders must be extremely vigilant about buying imported electrical, electronic and mechanical goods, some of which have proved highly danger-ous in the past. They also have to be careful about goods assembled in the UK but containing parts produced in, say, the Far East. They may be forewarned by the number of such products which have been subject to product recalls by reputable British manufacturers.

DATA PROTECTION ACT 1984

If you have the time and patience to read the eight booklets in your registration pack you may discover what this Act is all about. It is probably quicker and safer to complete the application forms and hope for the best, paying £20 for the privilege.

The following are the seven data protection principles by which registered data users must comply. Personal data shall be:

1   Collected and processed fairly and lawfully.
2   Held only for lawful purposes described in the register entry.
3   Used only for those purposes and disclosed only to those people described in the register entry.
4   Adequate, relevant and not excessive in relation to the purposes for which they are held.
5   Accurate and, where necessary, kept up to date.
6   Held no longer than is necessary for the registered purpose.
7   Protected by proper security.

The idea is that if you hold data about other people on a computer (other than for household purposes) you are obliged to disclose this to the Data Protection Registrar. If a member of the public wishes to have a printout of this information they can pay a fee of £10 and request it. A list of the 200 000 or so organizations that hold personal data is contained in the Register, copies of which are held in 171 libraries nationwide.

The problem is: how do you know whose computer holds information about you? This may be obvious in the case of, say, an employer or a bank, but what about the direct response business? Customer information may be on scores of unknown databases, making the Act unworkable.

However, the advertising and direct response industries have made serious efforts to unravel the mysteries of data protection. The British List Brokers Association has issued a comprehensive guidance note, *Implications of the Data Protection Act for Direct Marketing/Direct Mailing.*

Most useful is the special *Code of Practice Covering the use of Personal Data for Advertising and Direct Marketing Purposes*, published in March 1987 by the Advertising Association, Abford House, 15 Wilton Road, London, SW1V 1NJ. The code provides an important link with the Mailing Preference Service.

Although users of automatically processed information were given until May 11, 1986 to register, this was somewhat unrealistic. Two years later it was clear that there were users who had never heard of the Act, while new users and new mailing lists are constantly coming into existence. Meanwhile, about a third of the complaints received by the Registrar are about unsolicited mail, which is not surprising since the bulk of direct mail is inevitably unsolicited!

Anyone who believes they should register, or who require further information (which will be supplied with forbidding generosity), should apply to: The Office of the Data Protection Registrar, Enquiry Service, Springfield House, Water Lane, Wilmslow, Cheshire SK9 5AX (telephone: 0625 535777).

The Act came into full operation on November 11, 1987.

DIRECT MAIL PRODUCERS ASSOCIATION CODE OF PRACTICE

34 Grand Avenue, London NI0 3BP (telephone: 01 734 0058)

The DMPA code was first published in 1972, and revised in 1975, 1981, 1983 and 1985. It lays down that members shall:

1   Undertake to promote the use and improve the status of direct mail as an advertising medium.
2   Set and maintain high standards, and ensure that the prestige of the Association and direct mail advertising is upheld.
3   Exercise reasonable care in entering upon commitments, and generally uphold and maintain the standards set by the Code of Advertising Practice and the Code of Sales Promotion Practice and, unless specifically exempt, to contribute to the levy as applying from time to time raised

by the Advertising Standards Board of Finance to fund the work of the Advertising Standards Authority. In particular, members will not mail or produce for mailing, literature or material which may be regarded as vulgar, dishonest, indecent, illegal or likely to cause offence in any way to recipients or to any other persons.

4 Report to the executive council approaches made to them of any direct mail project which falls, or seems to fall, below the standards described in section 3 above. The report will be recorded. Members will be advised of the report for their guidance.

5 Not make exaggerated claims concerning the accuracy of lists or facilities available.

6 Not mail at rebate rates without the express agreement of clients.

7 Subscribe to the Mail Preference Service if they own, broke or rent consumer lists.

DIRECT MAIL SERVICES STANDARDS BOARD

26 Eccleston Street, London SW1W 9PY (telephone: 01 824 8651)

The Direct Mail Services Standards Board was established in 1983 with Post Office support to promote improvements in the ethical and professional standards of the direct mail advertising industry. The Board runs a recognition system for direct mail agencies which adhere to the British Code of Advertising Practice and other relevant codes, and have been scrutinized by the Board's staff. They receive from it a commission on their postage bill. Advertisers are encouraged to use agencies recognized by the DMSSB. More than 150 agencies are so recognized; a booklet listing such agencies is available on request.

The Board and its activities are not directly visible to the consumer: it deals mainly with advertisers and their agencies. Where consumer complaints occur, they continue to be directed to the CAP Committee, and those upheld by the ASA are referred to the Board for action if a recognized agency is involved.

MAIL ORDER PROTECTION SCHEME

16 Tooks Court, London EC4A 1LB

Some publishers operate their own 'reader protection' scheme, vetting direct response advertisers to make sure that readers' complaints are avoided, as these reflect on the publishers' own good reputation. It is usually necessary to check that the advertiser has the means of supplying ordered goods within a reasonable time, such as 28 days. Publishers

THE NATIONAL NEWSPAPER

MOPS

MAIL ORDER PROTECTION SCHEME

MAIL ORDER AM I PROTECTED?

★ Can I send my money with confidence?
★ What if the advertiser ceases to trade?
★ Will I get my money back?
★ Who can I turn to for advice?
★ What is MOPS?

Since 1975 the Newspaper Publishers Association's Mail Order Protection Scheme (MOPS) has operated to protect readers of national newspapers from financial loss when a mail order advertiser ceases to trade.

Mail Order advertisements within this newspaper requiring payment to be sent in direct response are approved under the terms of the Mail Order Protection Scheme (MOPS).

The scheme does not cover certain types of advertisements including classified announcements and purchases from catalogues and brochures.

Members of the Scheme may, if they wish, display the initials MOPS in their advertisements.

If in doubt, write to the MOPS office in London.

REMEMBER – MOPS EXISTS FOR YOUR PROTECTION AND SATISFACTION.

Full details of MOPS and the excluded categories of advertising can be easily obtained by sending a stamped and addressed envelope to:
The National Newspaper Mail Order Protection Scheme (MOPS), 16 Tooks Court, London EC4A 1LB.

ORDER WITH CONFIDENCE

also seek to discourage advertisers who may not order goods until they themselves have received orders and payment: in the past, advertisers who did this went bankrupt because prices had gone up and they could not supply at their advertised prices.

A number of publishers subscribe to the national newspaper MOPS service, and announce this in their publications with display advertisements. It is sponsored by the Newspaper Publishers' Association (representing national newspapers) and the Periodical Publishers' Association (representing magazines). The scheme protects readers when buying through display advertisements in British newspapers or magazines. Advertisers are vetted and have to pay into a central fund which is used to compensate a reader if an advertiser goes bankrupt.

However, the scheme does not cover classified advertisements or purchases from catalogues and brochures which may, of course, have been obtained in response to a press advertisement.

MAILING PREFERENCE SERVICE

1 New Burlington Street, London W1X 0FD

This service is sponsored by the Association of Mail Order Publishers, the British Direct Marketing Association, the British List Brokers Association, the Direct Mail Producers Association, the Mail Order Traders Association, and the Mail Users Association.

The Mailing Preference Service seeks to encourage the highest ethical standards in direct marketing, to streamline effective mailing and administration, and to help its members observe fully the spirit of the Data Protection Act.

It does this by enabling consumers to have their names and home addresses excluded from – or added to – mailing lists controlled or used by members of MPS. The service is entirely free to the public. As a result of media comment or advertising by MPS, members of the public complete and return personal applications stating their wish to be excluded from – or added to – current mailing lists. Forms for this purpose are available from the service.

These names are then put on the MPS consumer file. The updated consumer file, showing all names to be added or excluded, is available quarterly to members in hard copy or tape form, depending on individual preference. Members then undertake in accordance with the rules of membership to exclude those names from, or add them to, the mailing lists they use.

The Mailing Preference Service is an integral part of the direct mail industry, and the Data Protection Registrar attaches the greatest importance to it as according well with the requirement for fair processing of personal data contained in the first of the seven data protection principles given earlier. It was established in 1983 by the direct marketing associations listed above with the full support of the Post Office to foster good relations between the industry and members of the general public. It was set up partly in anticipation of the complex requirements of data protection legislation, and partly to meet the industry's growing awareness that criticism of direct mail – even if unjustified – harmed the image, the long-term interests and the effective operation of the whole industry.

Lists cleaned against the MPS consumer file remain more up to date and more cost-effective. The waste, cost and administrative effort of sending often expensive mailings to individuals who have no wish to receive them, and of dealing with their subsequent complaints, are removed. Conversely, names of those from whom a positive response can be expected are added to existing lists. But, along with the financial savings the mailer can directly make in time and materials, MPS itself makes an essential contribution to the standing, reputation and public image of the industry.

Membership by annual subscription is open to all organizations involved in direct marketing and direct mailing to consumers. Those who subscribe to the service agree to abide by and conform with rules of membership.

Mailers – subscribers who themselves mail direct to the public

– pay a subscription based on their total addressed promotional annual mailing volume. The subscription year is March 1 to February 28, and mailers who join after the start of the year pay a subscription on a pro rata basis, related to the number of MPS quarterly updates to be received.

Suppliers – list owners, brokers, agencies, mailing houses and so on – pay a standard subscription to cover a share of the administration costs of MPS.

The MPS is a non-profit-making organization.

18   Export direct marketing

Are there overseas markets which you can reach? Some overseas sales may be derived from off-the-page advertising in British publications which also circulate overseas. If so, any special conditions, such as airmail postage or payment in sterling on a UK bank, will need to be set out very clearly in your advertisement.

When booking advertisement space you must check on overseas circulation. Some journals, like *The Economist*, allow you to advertise in particular editions. This may be important if you do not want to advertise in, say, the USA to which the bulk of that journal's circulation goes.

If you are selling important products, what is the extent of your franchise? It might be UK or European only and you cannot accept orders from other parts of the world. Be careful not to attract orders you cannot service, even to the extent of stating the limitations of your sales area.

But if you want the bonus of overseas circulation, check on the circulation list. This may be a deciding factor in choosing media. Remember, many British publications sell copies abroad, and some specialist journals depend on an international circulation. A number of newspapers and magazines, thanks to satellites, are printed simultaneously in far-off parts of the globe and may cover all continents, certainly Europe, North America, South East Asia and the Far East.

There can be certain problems. Response to ads may arrive weeks, months and even years after publication. In countries where magazines are scarce they are often kept or passed on. You may be out of stock, or the price may have changed, by the time you receive the order and payment. Postage rates may have gone up.

You will also have to be prepared to pack protectively, to be familiar with postage rates for different countries, and to know the kind and number of custom forms. But especially, careful packing is vital, bearing in mind how packages are roughly handled scores of times by the Post Office and transporters. This may mean extra cost which has to be included in the price. When you see the shattered state in which packages arrive in the UK you will realize that a very special effort is necessary when packing for overseas customers. For some peculiar reason, people are very optimistic about the fate of postal packages.

Perhaps you want to insure parcels, but not all countries accept insurance. Despatches overseas are therefore more complex and time consuming than inland despatches, but this is not to say that the business is not worth while. I have been selling to 70 countries for many years.

OVERSEAS DIRECT MAIL OR PRESS ADVERTISING

Direct mail is in many ways the best medium for seeking overseas sales, for it is both *economical* and *controllable* – which are not entirely the same thing. It is more economical because the spend is infinitely less than buying space in numerous publications. This depends on whether or not you can find press media which will reach a large number of the right prospects. To find out it is worth buying a copy of *Benn's Media Directory* which, in its UK edition, gives profiles of thousands of journals. So, if you are in the educational market and want to sell to the Arab market, which is paying a lot of attention to education, you will find that *Middle East Education and Training* has the following profile:

> Circulated free to ministries of education, university libraries, key educationalists and trainers and specialist agencies. News, product reviews and reports on all areas of teaching and industrial training throughout the Arab world.
> Readership: senior academics, planners, training insti-

tutions and specialist commercial suppliers who are resident in the Middle East.

Ideally, you should obtain specimen copies of magazines you think useful, and see who is advertising in them. In my business I find that one particular publication which sells in 40 countries is a very profitable advertising medium.

CHOOSING COUNTRIES

The easiest way to conduct overseas direct marketing is to concentrate on English-speaking countries. These can be big ones like the USA, Canada, Australia and South Africa, or those which were formerly British colonies. They can range from huge subcontinents like India to small states like Malawi or Mauritius. There are also countries where English is well spoken as a second language, usually for business purposes, and they can include places like Cameroon, Thailand, Indonesia and the Arab states.

You must choose your countries carefully, but there is no reason why you cannot spread your mailing internationally. I have won business from some surprising places, such as Brunei, Curaçao, Ethiopia, Nepal, Sarawak and Tahiti.

MAILING LISTS FOR OVERSEAS USE

There are sources of international mailing lists such as Lists Media International of Slough, or you may prefer to compile your own.

A very useful source of addresses is the series of *Major Companies* directories published for different parts of the world by Graham and Trotman. These mostly annual volumes give company profiles and the names of top personnel. There are also specific international trade direct-ories such as the *Bankers' Almanac*. In the *Financial Times* series of international yearbooks there are editions on industrial companies, oil and gas, hotels, insurance and other subjects from which lists can be compiled.

No doubt there is such a directory concerning your

particular trade or type of customer. There are also international membership directories of professional bodies which have members worldwide. The addresses will be found in the extensive directories section of *Benn's Media Directory*, where scores of directories and yearbooks for compiling UK mailing lists will be found.

If you are interested in particular cities, there are trade directories for most of the world's large cities, and there are, of course, *Yellow Pages* throughout the world. For Europe, a useful book is the *European Directory of Marketing Information Sources*. A reference book, *International Mailing Lists: how to use them, where to find them*, costs £21.95 from Royal Mail International Letters – see address later in this chapter under 'Post Office'.

PECULIARITIES OF OVERSEAS MARKETS

In many countries, and not necessarily because postal services are bad, direct mail is rare if not unknown. Your mail shot may be an extremely welcome novelty, and mail from abroad may excite the curiosity it would not enjoy in the UK. How can you exploit these advantages?

A sales letter may be welcome simply because it is a letter, but here care is necessary to give it the appearance of a legitimate letter. Some of the clumsy, verbose and over-persuasive, printed and sometimes miniaturized efforts already criticized will be useless. The courtesies have to be observed, and content needs to be informative and credible.

People who are reading in a second language may do little reading in English, and will not relish being overwhelmed by long letters. They may also be sceptical about advertising, and easily put off by excessively persuasive copy. This may be because advertising is not controlled in their countries, and they have learned to mistrust advertising claims. So, while your mail shot may well be a novelty to them, it must not lack credibility.

These are points which have to be studied very carefully, because what goes in Britain is liable to be unsuitable in countries where advertising is less commonplace or social values are very different. A lot of British-type high-pressure advertising can be offensive or unbelievable abroad. Modern susceptibilities have to be scrupulously observed.

Having said that, certain appeals and words that may lack credibility in the UK will be more effective in some parts of the developing world, especially Africa. Appeals to power and wealth, or the use of words like magic or magical, may be very acceptable.

The initial appearance of the shot can be important. An airmail envelope will identify its foreign origin. Although there are special rate mailing services when envelopes are franked, you may consider it worth the extra trouble and cost to fix actual postage stamps, such as the large pictorial ones, to effect a more personal and interesting correspondence. The extra cost may induce extra attention. Even in a foreign business house which does receive a large mail, the envelope bearing the foreign stamp may be the first to be opened. There are therefore some powerful psychological considerations to think about here. Too much direct mail is rendered dull before the envelope is even opened, and this can be fatal overseas.

The language of colour has been discussed elsewhere, but it is worth mentioning here if you use printed envelopes. They can be printed in different colours for different parts of the world, say, green for the Arab or other Muslim states, red for the East. Coloured envelopes can also be used.

There are also certain attitudes of mind to be observed, particularly regarding pricing strategy. In many overseas countries no one expects to pay the full price, and there is always a 'last price'. You may therefore find it wise to decide on your final price, increase it and offer discounts for cash, quantities or quick response, adopting a technique that appeals to the bazaar or merchant mind which insists on haggling. However, for Europe discounts must be genuine ones or you may be breaking the law.

COPY FOR FOREIGN MARKETS

The copy needs to be written even more skilfully than for the home market, and if this is overlooked you will be inviting disaster. If you are unfamiliar with overseas markets – which is to be expected, because the British tend to be incredibly insular – you need to realize very quickly that they have certain unusual characteristics.

The English language is exquisitely rich. It has some perplexing contradictions in pronunciation (such as the *verb* refuse and the *noun* refuse), and it has a vocabulary range which is often squandered by its British users. There is also English idiom like 'over the hill', and slang which changes rapidly, which can bemuse foreigners. Overseas people who may speak English may read very little and write even less. This is a fact well known to examiners who set papers taken by students abroad. Consequently, the vocabularies of foreigners are bound to be limited. It is not that they are less well educated, but that they use fewer English words. To say this is to be realistic, not condescending.

When writing copy for sales letters and sales literature intended for English-speaking overseas buyers, the following guidelines should be observed:

1 Use short words of Anglo-Saxon origin wherever possible.
2 Use short sentences and paragraphs, avoiding complex sentences and rambling parentheses.
3 Avoid using words which have different meanings either in the English language itself (such as stone, gorge, vent, box) or overseas, or even ones with similar sound but different spelling and/or meaning, like hoard and horde or plane and plain. For example, in some countries a single cigarette is called a stick, all drinks may be called tea, while children may be called babies for several years after what we regard as babyhood. A baby car may be thought to be a toy car. A saloon car can be confused with a car showroom. Ambiguity can abound!
4 If you are selling in countries, such as in the East or Australia, where people are confronted by both English English and American English, beware of terms which have different or contrary meanings or totally different terms are used. When is a tub a barrel or a bath, or when is

confectionery a sweet or a candy? A British housewife goes shopping but an American housewife goes marketing. We broadcast but Americans air. A lot depends on whether they have read British or American books, where they were educated, or which English language newspapers or magazines they read. This may also affect the way they spell – tyre or tire, centre or center? A road show in Britain goes by road, but in the USA by railroad (not railway). If you are writing for the North American market you will have to translate into American English, and you will need an American English dictionary.

5   Try to think of everything your prospect needs to know if he is to respond. He has to trust you and be absolutely convinced if he is going to make a cash payment to a stranger thousands of miles away. Your copy must therefore be foolproof. It is highly unlikely that they will pick up a phone and ask for something to be explained more clearly. Everything must be perfectly clear in the first place. For example, if you were promoting a conference it would be sensible to print a map showing the accessibility of the location.

6   Establish your credentials. However well known you are in the UK, you will probably be unknown overseas. The date when you were established, lists of customers, testimonials, membership of trade associations, official recognitions and similar evidence of permanent, successful trading are worth including.

7   Make order forms and reply coupons absolutely specific regarding country. Don't just print 'address'. Many British and other towns have their counterparts elsewhere in the world. There is an Edmonton in Canada, a Box Hill in Australia, an Athens and a Paris in the USA, and Aberdeens in Hong Kong and elsewhere. Thank goodness Salisbury has been renamed Harare in Zimbabwe!

You therefore have to take a Martian's view of the world when writing copy for overseas sales material. You may not be right all the time, but you can be careful. All you have to do is pretend to be your distant prospect who has never heard of you, even if your name is Rothschild, and ask yourself exactly what you need to know if you are going to send money to a stranger.

PAYMENT

Cash with order is the safest method of conducting overseas mail order business. You may be asked to supply pro forma invoices so that application can be made to a central bank for permission to export sterling. With so many currency fluctuations, and with bank charges on converting foreign currency, it is usually best to accept sterling only. *This should be made very clear on the order form.* Some customers, unaccustomed to sending money abroad, may think they can pay local currency to your local agent, or that you have a local bank account. This may be the case but, if it is not, the order form must emphasize that payment has to be made to you in the UK in sterling.

There are some countries where it is difficult to get exchange control permission to export sterling, and others where deflation and the poor exchange rate make it prohibitive to buy sterling. Normally you will have no reason for leaving money with an agent or a bank, with little chance of getting the money transferred to Britain. Consequently, there are some countries to avoid. Nigeria is certainly one, unless customers have some means of making payment outside Nigeria. This may be possible with a multinational or with a company which trades abroad and has credit in Britain, Europe or the USA. But don't give credit just because there is a big name on the letterheading, not even to a government department. If they send the cash you can send the goods, but if you work the other way round you may never see the cash.

In the Third World the British are regarded as millionaires who can afford to supply free gifts. People in these countries can be more naive than dishonest. Also, if your order form is clearly worded you will avoid lengthy and costly correspondence.

It may also be wise to insist that enquiries, let alone orders, are signed by a person with authority to conduct business and pay bills. Subordinates are capable of issuing enquiries or orders without such authority, and they can be time and money wasters.

TRANSLATIONS

If you are producing mail shots in foreign languages, the translations must be perfect. Some English words can translate into absurdities if they have a variety of meanings, are technical jargon, or there is no precise foreign equivalent.

There are two ways to perfect translations. First, the translator should be given definitions of special terms. Second, it is best if the translator is a native working in his own language. A method adopted by EIBIS International (who specialize in distributing PR stories to the overseas press) is to have the translation retranslated into English and to compare this version with the original English version. In any case, it is best to use simple English, with a minimum of jargon and no idiomatic expressions or puns.

Translated copy may occupy different volumes of space, and allowance for this must be made when designing print. A German translation may need up to a third more space than the original English version.

You also need to be sure that your printer has either foreign type or foreign accents. There are printers who specialize in setting in, say, Arabic, Chinese or Japanese characters, but laser printers often have limited founts.

The IPMC company of London, which also has associated companies in Canada, the Netherlands and the USA, offers a 'one-stop shopping' service for translations and foreign print. Work is checked at each stage by a foreign national of the relevant language. Whatever the language, typesetting is available with the correct accents, the right hyphenization, and in the appropriate typographical style.

LEGAL CONSIDERATIONS

Some of the special techniques common to UK mailings may be illegal in certain countries, particularly in Europe where sales promotional gimmicks may be banned. Words like 'free', 'exclusive' and 'new' must be avoided unless they are true, while in Germany and some Scandinavian countries free gifts are illegal because they are considered unfair competition and even capable of exerting unfair moral pressure. To be safe, it is best to make straightforward sales offers. The restraints, or lack of them, must be considered closely, but generally the high-pressure mailings so familiar in Britain can lead to legal problems overseas.

If you are using mailing lists supplied by overseas sources you may have to identify the list broker. It may therefore be less troublesome to compile your own lists from directories and other sources, as suggested at the beginning of this chapter.

MAILING SERVICES

There are both Post Office and private overseas mailing services, and these are now briefly introduced. Fuller details and quotations should be obtained from each service. Quotations can be very competitive; TNT, for instance, offers a saving of around 50 per cent on printed paper mailings.

Post Office

Airmail printed papers, marked 'printed paper rate' and unsealed (unless permission to seal has been obtained), enjoy normal air mail letter service.

Surface printed papers can be sent similarly but obviously to more distant places; this can be very much slower.

Airstream service is international for minimum quantities of 250.

Airstream print Europe is for large mailing of presorted printed paper to Europe, on a kilogram basis.

Accelerated surface post is a useful and economical service for large quantities of printed paper. It has a surface mail service within the UK and the country of destination, but air carriage between the two countries.

Airmail printed paper contract is for senders of large quantities of printed paper to countries outside Europe.

International business reply service has a licence fee of £20 and a charge of 25p per reply returned.

From Royal Mail International Letters, Room 320, 52 Grosvenor Gardens, London SW1W 0YA you can obtain a free information pack on international direct mail.

TNT Mailfast

Using its own collection service and international transport system, TNT specializes in international mailing. It uses a number of overseas mailing centres from which it redistributes mail to nearby countries. For instance, the Miami centre redistributes to the Caribbean, Central and South America; the Hong Kong centre redistributes to the Far East, India, Pakistan, China, Japan, Hong Kong, Indonesia and the Philippines. TNT Mailfast collects unstamped mail, sorts it, and flies it to overseas centres where it is posted locally in the normal way. There are kilogram rates for mail units under or over 60 grams, to Europe or zones A, B and C. The sender sorts mail into zones, notes the number of items per zone, bundles mail by zones, and with the consignment note bags it for collection in provided sacks. A TNT van collects the sacks.

Pharos Distribution Services Ltd

This is a different kind of service. It consolidates mail to take advantage of two of the Post Office services described above –Airstream (Europe/rest of the world) and accelerated surface post. The advantages of the Pharos service over dealing direct with the Post Office are that there are no minimum weights or quantities, no documentation and no weight steps. Pharos rates are less than Post Office rates if applicable charges are made for collection, stamping and sorting. Clients may use the Pharos PPI (Printed Postage Impression).

Mailflight

This is another international mailing service, with mail sorted down to post towns, which has been developed with the postal authorities in Britain, the USA and Holland. Mail can be delivered to the Bedford centre, or collected from the sender. Time is saved by the presorting procedure before the mail is sent to overseas destinations. This eliminates the normal Post Office procedures of UK sorting into countries, and local sorting into regions and towns. Thus, on arrival at countries of destination, your mail goes straight into the postal delivery networks.

The addresses of services mentioned in this chapter are given at the end of the book.

International Linkline (0800)

In Chapter 13 reference was made to Linkline 0800. There is also International 0800 which enables customers to dial free phone calls direct to you. No special lines or additional equipment are required, and the system can encourage overseas buyers to make enquiries or place orders. It can overcome the need to have overseas sales offices, agents or sales staff and so becomes an excellent form of direct response marketing.

The system is being expanded, but at the time of writing International 0800 is available from Australia, Denmark, West Germany, France, the Netherlands, Sweden, Switzerland and the United States.

International mail box

The Telecom Gold electronic mail box service described in Chapter 13 can also be extended internationally, since the American Dialcom system is available in many countries. You can thus mail any Dialcom mail box anywhere in the world. It is especially useful for sending large-text communications very quickly to overseas customers. This, of course, lends itself mostly to mailings to small selected groups of buyers rather than to large-scale shots.

19 Direct mail marketing associations

The codes of practice of a number of organizations concerned with the ethics of direct response marketing have been outlined in Chapter 17. This chapter introduces the trade bodies which service the direct mail and direct marketing industries. Membership of such associations, or use of companies which are in membership, will help the direct marketer to perform efficiently and professionally. He can benefit from the experience, knowledge and expertise which, collectively, these bodies represent.

ASSOCIATION OF MAIL ORDER PUBLISHERS

1 New Burlington Street, London W1X 1FD (telephone: 01 437 0706)

This is the trade association of those companies engaged in the direct selling of books, magazines and music products. It was founded in 1970, and its principal aim is to represent the views of the members in general matters affecting the industry. This occurs in several different ways: for example when the government has legislation in mind, or when new directives are considered or in draft in the European Economic Commission, and in discussions with the Post Office and other industry associations in direct marketing, publishing and so on.

The Association is represented on the Code of Advertising Practice Committee, the Advertising Association and its standing committees and the National Book Committee. The Association is available for consultation by members on questions affecting their legal position. The Association also has links with those departments of local government responsible for enforcement of laws regulating trade.

Its members subscribe to its self-regulatory Code of Practice which is administered by the Mail Order Publishers Authority, a body separate from the Association and with an independent chairman. The public is free to send complaints to the Authority about the treatment they have had from members; provided the complainants identify themselves and make a written statement of their complaints, the Authority will investigate. The code was reissued in 1977 with the approval of the Director-General of Fair Trading, who is given an annual report on the working of the code.

Membership comprises full members, associate members and affiliates. The first two consist of mail order publishers themselves, and the difference is one of size. The affiliates consist of companies providing services to the members: for example, advertising agencies. All full members are automatically represented on the executive committee, while associates are represented by two persons, and affiliates by one. They are elected annually.

In its more than 17 years' existence, the Association of Mail Order Publishers has performed effectively as a trade association and lobby, and can claim a string of successes in negotiating with government departments, consumer agencies, legislators and other interested parties. Perhaps the best indicator of what has been achieved comes in comparing the conditions of mail order (direct response) and direct mail in the UK with those in other countries. Although companies may at times feel hampered and hamstrung, the industry is a lot freer than they are, particularly in the fields of privacy, use of premia and wholehearted commitment to the principles of self-regulation.

Publications include bulletins, occasional papers, *AMOP News*, and an annual report to members.

BRITISH DIRECT MARKETING ASSOCIATION

Grosvenor Gardens House, Grosvenor Gardens, London SW1W 0BS (telephone: 01 630 7322)

This is the only trans-industry, multitrade association for all types of direct marketing within the UK. The BDMA was founded in 1976, and represents its members' views to government and other official bodies on matters affecting their operations. It runs the industry's major conferences, seminars and other events. In conjunction with the Post Office the Association administers the BDMA/Royal Mail direct marketing awards for excellence. It provides a free legal/commercial advisory service for its members.

The BDMA sponsors a diploma course which is conducted at colleges such as Kingston Polytechnic, Bristol Polytechnic, and the Polytechnic of Central London. The 30-week evening course leads to an examination and the BDMA Diploma in Direct Marketing.

There are some 400 members. They come from both companies which use direct marketing to promote their own goods and services, and from those who provide services to the direct marketing industry.

The BDMA operates its own Code of Practice and Telephone Marketing Guidelines, and members must also adhere to the British Code of Advertising Practice and the British Code of Sales Promotion Practice, the latter two codes being administered by the Advertising Standards Authority.

Publications include the quarterly *BDMA News* and *Liveline*. A members' handbook is also published.

BRITISH LIST BROKERS ASSOCIATION

Premier House, 150 Southampton Road, London WC1B 3AL (telephone: 01 278 0236)

Representing the majority of British list brokers, the BLBA was set up in 1983 so that as the direct mail advertising medium grew, list brokers – a vital element in the direct mail equation – should ensure that their own standards of service remained at the highest possible levels.

Membership consists of full members, who are companies which derive a significant part of their business activity from the regular broking of mailing lists; associate members, who are list owners, list managers, service bureaux and other related industries; and overseas members, who come within any of the previously mentioned categories.

The brokers' relationship with direct response agencies, computer bureaux, list owners and direct houses is such that the members agreed that the second tier of associate membership should be introduced. Coupled with this, the technological advances introduced into direct mail advertising made it imperative that brokers worked closely with related businesses to ensure cohesion and understanding of each other's problems and aspirations. This included giving advice to users of these services.

The BLBA publishes information about its members and the services they offer; a glossary of list terms; an industry definitions folder; a Trading Practice Guide; and standard terms and conditions of list rental and trading. It publishes a useful statement on net names for those who are volume users of third-party mailing lists but who carry out a merge/purge exercise to de-duplicate lists used simultaneously. In general this means that a client pays full rental price for at least 85 per cent of the names supplied, but pays the full rental price if 90–95 per cent of the list is mailed (see Chapter 4).

DIRECT MAIL PRODUCERS ASSOCIATION

34 Grand Avenue, London N10 3BP (telephone: 01 883 7229)

Representing the production side of the direct mail industry, this specialist trade body has 110 members and publishes a directory in which detailed descriptions of their services are printed.

The Association is a member of the Advertising Association and the Mail Users Association and enjoys reciprocal membership of the European Direct Marketing Association and the US Direct Marketing Association. It subscribes to CAM and the Direct Marketing Centre, organizes an annual week-long executive residential direct mail course, and sponsors the Direct Marketing Fair and is represented on its advisory committee.

The Association operates a Code of Practice.

DIRECT MAIL SALES BUREAU

14 Floral Street, Covent Garden, London WC2E 9RR (telephone: 01 379 7531)

Set up by the Post Office and the chief practitioners in direct mail in 1985, the Bureau's objective is the provision of a central single point of access to the whole medium.

With the help of the Consumer Location System database, or through analysis of their own customers' records, advertisers can communicate directly with their existing or potential customers. The Bureau also offers a planning and executive centre.

The Bureau helps in the strategic planning of mailing lists, print and production, fulfilment, pre- and post-campaign evaluation on a 'one-stop shopping' basis of one order, one invoice. Although this is a service particularly favoured by advertising agencies, it is available direct to clients.

The Bureau also publishes a useful Planner's Guide which is described at the end of this chapter.

DIRECT MAIL SERVICES STANDARDS BOARD

See Chapter 17 for a description of the Board.

OTHER SOURCES OF INFORMATION

Cost-Effective Direct Marketing, Collectors' Books Ltd, Cirencester, Glos. GL7 1BR. Based on 35 years' experience, this is Christian Brann's classic on the subject.

Creative Handbook, The, British Media Publications, Windsor Court, East Grinstead, West Sussex RH19 1XA. This is a 750-page annual portfolio/directory of British creative talents, richly illustrated with full-colour samples of artwork/photography, with an extensive directory of names and addresses.

Direct Mail Databook, Gower Publishing Company Ltd, Gower House, Croft Road, Aldershot, Hampshire GU11 3HR. First published in 1973, this reference work for direct mail users has had a succession of revised editions. Contains more than 450 pages in A4 format and is edited by Leslie J. Goodwin in association with Mardev Ltd.

Direct Response Direct Marketing Guide, 4 Market Place, Hertford SG14 1EB. This annual supplement in *Direct Response* magazine provides a classified guide to every category of direct response service and supplier.

Guide to Effective Direct Mail, The Post Office Direct Mail Department, Room 195, Post Office Headquarters, 33 Grosvenor Place, London SW1X 1PX (telephone: 01 245 7031). An excellent, simple and informative 'how to do it' booklet for direct mail users, which is available free of charge.

Planner's Guide to Direct Mail, Direct Mail Sales Bureau, 14 Floral Street, London WC2E 9RR (telephone: 01 379 7531). This introductory guide to the use of direct mail is available free of charge. It has a very interesting section on consumer attitudes to direct mail, and explains planning and testing, postal campaigns, mailing lists, and Royal Mail services.

Bibliography

BOOKS

Cost-Effective Direct Marketing, Christian Brann. Collectors Books, Cirencester.

Desk Top Publishing from A to Z, Irene Athanasopoulos and Rebecca Kutlin. McGraw-Hill, Maidenhead, Berkshire, 1986.

Direct Mail Databook. Gower, Aldershot, 1987.

Guide to Effective Direct Mail. Post Office Direct Mail Department, Room 195, Post Office Headquarters, 33 Grosvenor Place, London SW1X 1PY.

Planner's Guide to Direct Mail, The. Direct Mail Sales Bureau, 14 Floral Street, London WC2E 9RR.

Successful Direct Marketing Methods, Bob Stone. Gower, Aldershot, 1987.

Successful Telemarketing, Bob Stone and John Wyman. Gower, Aldershot, 1987.

Using Pagemaker for the PC, Martin and Carole Matthews. McGraw-Hill, Maidenhead, Berkshire, 1987.

Using the Microcomputer in Marketing, Lynn and Stephen Parkinson. McGraw-Hill, Maidenhead, Berkshire, 1987.

DIRECTORIES

Advertiser's Annual, Windsor Court, East Grinstead House, East Grinstead, W. Sussex RH19 1XA.

Benn's Media Directory, PO Box 20, Sovereign Way, Tonbridge, Kent TN9 1RQ.

Creative Handbook, The, Windsor Court, East Grinstead House, East Grinstead, W. Sussex RH19 1XA.

European Directory of Marketing Information Sources, Euromonitor Publications Ltd, 87–8 Turnmill Street, London EC1M 5QU.

JOURNALS

Campaign (weekly), 22 Lancaster Gate, London W2 3LY.
Direct Response (monthly), 4 Market Place, Hertford SG14 1EB.
Marketing (weekly), 22 Lancaster Gate, London W2 3LY.
Marketing Week (weekly), St Giles House, 49–50 Poland Street, London W1V 4AX.

Useful addresses

These addresses include those of organizations and firms mentioned in this book.

BRITISH TELECOM

British Telecom Marketing Services, Freepost, Bristol BS1 6GZ.

Linkline Marketing (0800), British Telecom, Intel House, 24 Southwark Bridge Road, London SE1 9HJ.

Telecom Gold Ltd, 60–68 St Thomas Street, London SE1 3QU.

DATA ANALYSIS SYSTEMS

CACI Market Analysis Division (ACORN), 59–62 High Holborn, London WC1 6DX.

CCN Systems Ltd (MOSAIC), Talbot House, Talbot Street, Nottingham NG1 6HS.

Consumer Location System (CLS), Direct Mail Sales Bureau, 14 Floral Street, London WC2E 9RR.

Demographic Profiles Ltd (Super Profiles), McIntyre House, Canning Place, Liverpool L1 8HY.

ICC Information Group Ltd, 28–42 Banner Street, London EC1Y 8QE.

Interactive Market Systems (TGI), Grosvenor Gardens House, Grosvenor Gardens, London SW1W 0BS.

Pinpoint Analysis Ltd (PIN), Mercury House, 117 Waterloo Road, London SE1 8UL.

DATABASES AND DATABASE SERVICES

AGB Sure Shots, Audit House, Field End Road, Eastcote, Ruislip, Middlesex HA9 4LT.

British Investors Database, Petersham House, 4th Floor, 57a Hatton Garden, London EC1N 8JD.

Control Marketing Ltd, 530 Purley Way, Croydon, Surrey CR0 4RE.

Databank Ltd, London House, Old Court Place, 26–40 Kensington High Street, London W8 4PF.

Datema, Colston Centre, Colston Avenue, Bristol BS1 4UH.

Dun's Marketing, Dun & Bradstreet International, 26–32 Clifton Street, London EC2P 2LY.

EMAP Direct, Abbot's Court, 34 Farrington Lane, London EC1R 3AU.

Inspectorate UCC, 344–50 Euston Road, London NW1 3BJ.

ListShop Ltd, Psycho-Demographic Database, The Business Village, Broomhill Road, London SW18 4JQ.

Mardev Ltd, 88–98 College Road, Harrow, Middlesex HA1 1AX.

Merit Direct Ltd, Conrad House, Birmingham Road, Stratford-upon-Avon, Warwickshire CV37 0AZ.

Pegasus Direct Marketing, 7–10 Old Bailey, London EC99 1AA.

Pippbrook Software Ltd, Pippbrook Mill, London Road, Dorking, Surrey RH4 1JE.

Printronic Corporation (UK) Ltd, 1 Endeavour Way, London, SW19 8UH.

Stonehart Direct Marketing Services, 57–61 Mortimer Street, London W1N 7TD.

TMC Data Base, Rhosili Road, Brackmills, Northampton NN4 0JE.

UCL Universal Computers Ltd, Great Western House, Station Approach, Taunton, Somerset TA1 0QW.

Valldata Services, Oakwood Spa Road, Melksham, Wiltshire SN12 7NP.

DESKTOP EDITING

Applitek (Wordsmith Publishing System), Felgate House, 6 Studland Street, London W6 0JS.

DIRECT MARKETING HOUSES, COMPUTER AND POSTCODING SERVICES

Amherst Direct Marketing, Amherst House, Ferring Street, Ferring, Worthing, W. Sussex, BN12 5JR.

Avon Direct Mail Services Ltd, PO Box 1, Portishead, Bristol BS90 9BR.

BTB Mailing Services Ltd, Unit 15, The Manton Centre, Manton Lane, Bedford MK41 7PX.

Capscan Ltd, 17 Elverton Street, London SW1P 2QG.

CCN Systems Ltd, Talbot House, Talbot Street, Nottingham NG1 5HF.

Centre-File Ltd (Nat-West Group), Direct Marketing Service, 75 Leman Street, London E1 8EX.

Credit & Data Marketing (CDMS) Services Ltd, JM Centre, Old Hall Street, Liverpool, L70 7AB.

DDM Advertising Ltd, 30 Eastbourne Terrace, London W2 6LG.

Direct Marketing Services, Retail Unit, 9 Montpelier Arcade, Cheltenham, Gloucestershire GL50 1SU.

Direct Response Media Ltd, Westminster House, Kew Road, Richmond, Surrey TW9 2ND.

DTI Group, Beech House, Betts Way, Crawley, W. Sussex RH10 1GB.

Holland & Partners Ltd, Ullswater Crescent, Coulsdon, Surrey CR3 2UU.

Laserlink/Istel Ltd, Isys House, PO Box 96, County Trading Estate, Watlington Road, Cowley, Oxford OX4 5LR.

Mail Centre, Osyth Close, Brackmills, Northampton NN4 0DY.

Mail Marketing (Bristol) Ltd/Datema, Springfield House, Princess Street, Bedminster, Bristol BS3 4EF.

Pegasus Direct Marketing Ltd, 7–10 Old Bailey, London EC99 1AA.

Precision Marketing International Ltd, 10 King Street, Covent Garden, London WC2E 8HN.

Printronic Corporation (UK) Ltd, 1 Endeavour Way, London SW19 8UX.

Southwark Computer Services, Becket House, 60–8 St Thomas Street, London SE7 3QU.

WWAV Computing Ltd, Kings House, Bond Street, Bristol BS1 3AE.

DOOR-TO-DOOR CIRCULAR DISTRIBUTORS

DMS Direct Ltd, 30 Bridge Road, Haywards Heath, W. Sussex RH16 1TU.

Marketforce Ltd, King House, 11 Westbourne Grove, London W2 4UR.

Network Letterbox Marketing, 5 Pemberton Road, London EC4A 3BA.

Royal Mail Household Delivery: local postal sales representative at GPO.

Target Distribution Services Ltd, 15 Hall Lane, Chingford, London E4 8HY.

ENVELOPE MAKERS AND PRINTERS

Envelopes International Ltd, Woodford Green, Essex 1G8 1BR.

Jet Envelope Printing Company, 64–65 Childers Street, London SE8 1SR.

Kitts Envelope Services, 53a De Beavoir Road, London N1 5AU.

Norman & Burgess, Edwards Lane, Speke, Liverpool L24 9HW.

Petrushkin Ltd, Petapak Works, Sugar House Lane, London E15 2QP.

Rutland Polythene, Wentworth Street, Ilkeston, Derbyshire DE7 5TF.

Sefton Polythene Ltd, Long Lane, Liver Industrial Estate, Liverpool 9.

SK Envelopes, 2–3 Bessemer Way, Harfreys Industrial Estate, Great Yarmouth, Norfolk NR31 0LX.

Southern Converters, Hewitt's Industrial Estate, Cranleigh, Surrey GU8 8LW.

Spicers Ltd, Sawston, Cambridge CB2 4JG.

Studio Promotion Envelopes Ltd, 97 Ewell Road, Surbiton, Surrey KT6 6AH.

Target Envelope Company, 27 Leyton Business Centre, Etloe Road, London E10 7BT.

Tompla UK Ltd, 48–50 Hartfield Road, London SW19 3TB.

LEGAL AND VOLUNTARY CONTROLS

Advertising Association, Abford House, 15 Wilton Road, London SW1V 1NS.

Advertising Standards Authority, Brook House, 2–16 Torrington Place, London WC1E 7HN.

British Direct Marketing Association Ltd, Grosvenor Gardens House, Grosvenor Gardens, London SW1W 0BS.

Data Protection Registrar, Springfield House, Water Lane, Wilmslow, Cheshire SK9 5AX.

Direct Mail Service Standards Board, 22 Eccleston Street, London SW1W 9PY.

Mailing Preference Service, 1 New Burlington Street, London W1X 1FD.

National Newspapers' Mail Order Protection Scheme Ltd, 16 Took's Court, London EC4A 1LB.

LIST BROKERS, MANAGERS

Financial Times Business Lists, Financial Times Business Information Ltd, 7th Floor, 50–54 Broadway, London SW1H 0DB.

Harrison List Broking Ltd, 35 Chapelside, Moscow Road, London W2 4LL.

IBIS, Waterside, Lowbell Lane, London Colney, St Albans, Herts AL2 1DX.

Jenkins Associates, 77 St John Street, London EC1M 4HH.

List Management Services Ltd, Nassau House, 122 Shaftesbury Avenue, London W1V.

Mailist Ltd, 1 White Ladies Road, Clifton, Bristol BS8 1NU.

Market Location, 17 Waterloo Place, Warwick Street, Leamington Spa, Warwickshire CV32 5LA.

Ralton Direct Media International, Stephenson Road, Groundwell, Swindon, SN2 5AN.

PHS Nelson Ltd, St Peters Road, Maidenhead, Berkshire SL6 6EZ.

SR List Management Ltd, SR House, Childers Street, London SE8 1SR.

OTHER MAIL DISTRIBUTION SERVICES

Pharos Distribution Services Ltd, 5–11 Lavington Street, London SE1 0NZ.

TNT Mailfast, Unit 6, Spitfire Way, Spitfire Way Industrial Estate, Hounslow, Middlesex TW5 9NW.

OVERSEAS SERVICES

BBC External Services, Export Liaison Unit, Bush House, Strand, London EC2B 4PH.

DHL Worldmail, 178–88 Great South West Road, Hounslow, Middlesex TW4 5BR.

EIBIS International, 3 Johnson's Court, Fleet Street, London EC4A 3EA.

Federal Express, 4th Floor, Ariston House, London Road, Loudwater, High Wycombe, Buckinghamshire HP11 1HF.

Hilal International (UK) Ltd, Al Halil Group (Middle East and Far East mailing lists), 3rd Floor, Regal House, London Road, Twickenham, Middlesex TW1 3QS.

IBIS, European List Brochure, Waterside, Lowbell Lane, London Colney, St Albans, Hertfordshire AL2 1DX.

Mail Resource, Unit 98G, Building 521, Heathrow Airport, Hounslow, Middlesex TW6 3TQ.

Mailflight Ltd, Woolfe House, Norse Road, Bedford MK41 0LF.

Mercury SDS Ltd, Unitair Centre, Great West Road, Feltham, Middlesex TW14 8NJ.

Parrot Mailing Co. Ltd, 157 Brent Road, Southall, Middlesex UB2 5LZ.

Royal Mail International Letters, Room 162, 33 Grosvenor Place, London SW1X 1EE.

TNT Mailfast, Unit 6, Spitfire Way, Spitfire Way Industrial Estate, Hounslow, Middlesex TW5 9NW.

Virgin International Print Distribution, Fleming Centre, Fleming Way, Crawley, W. Sussex RH10 7YH.

World Innovators (US mailing lists), 72 Park Street, New Canaan, Connecticut 06840, USA.

POSTCODE MAPS

Bartholomew & Sons Ltd, 12 Duncan Street, Edinburgh EH9 1TA.

Geographer A–Z Maps Co. Ltd, Vestry Road, Sevenoaks, Kent TN14 5EP.

Geographia Ltd, 65 Fleet Street, London EC4Y 1PE.

Stanford Ltd, 12–14 Long Acre, London WC2E 9LP.

PRINTERS

Aquaprint Ltd, Apsley Industrial Estate, Kents Avenue, Hemel Hempstead, Hertfordshire.

Broad-Response, Jesse Broad Ltd, Atlantic Street, Broadheath, Altrincham, Cheshire WA14 5EB.

Crawford's Computing, Laser Printing, Binns Road, Liverpool L17 9NG.

Imagen Ltd, Laser Printing, 24 Quebec Way, Surrey Quays, Rotherhithe, London SE16 1LF.

PRODUCTION PRODUCTS, SERVICES, GIMMICKS

Dobson & Crowther, Llangollen, Clwyd LL20 8AE.

Howitt Promotions, Barlock Road, Basford, Nottingham NG6 0FJ.

Hunterprint Group PLC, Saxon Way East, Oakley Way Industrial Park, Corby, Northamptonshire NN18 9EX.

Pinewood Label Systems Ltd, The Stables, Old Charlton Road, Shepperton, Middlesex TW17 8AT.

Scriptomatic Ltd (labelling machines), Scriptomatic House, Torrington Park, London N12 9SU.

Waddington & Ledger Ltd, Syke Ing Mills, Syke Lane, Dewsbury WF12 8HZ.

Waterlow Ltd, Direct Mail Products, George Street, Dunstable, Bedfordshire LU6 1BR.

ROYAL MAIL SERVICES

Intelpost (100 UK Intelpost centres linking fax owners, telex users, and microcomputer users with 30 countries), Royal Mail Marketing, 33 Grosvenor Place, London SW1X 1PX.

Introductory Offers to First-Time Users, Post Office Direct Mail Section, Room 195, 33 Grosvenor Place, London SW1X 1EE.

Letter Discount Services for Businessmen, Royal Mail Marketing Department, Room 195, Postal Headquarters, 33 Grosvenor Place, London SW1X 1EE.

Optical Character Recognition, Royal Mail Letters, Room 137, 33 Grosvenor Place, London SW1X 1EE.

Post Office Direct Mail Section, Room 195, 33 Grosvenor Place, London, SW1X 1EE.

Postcode Portfolio, Room 380, Postal Headquarters, London SW1X 1PX.

Printed Postage Impressions, Room 137, Postal Headquarters, 33 Grosvenor Place, London SW1X 1EE.

Royal Mail Household Delivery: local postal sales representative at GPO.

Royal Mail Marketing Department, Room 195, Postal Headquarters, 33 Grosvenor Place, London SW1X 1EE.

TELEMARKETING

Answering Ltd, 11 Rosemont Road, London NW3 6NG.

Business Extension, 7 Kenrick Place, Baker Street, London W1H 3FF.

Datacross Ltd, Lloyds Empire Buildings, 286 High Street, Connah's Quay, Deeside CH5 4DJ.

Directline Telemarketing, 91 Wimpole Street, London W1M
7DA.

Phonesell, Pembroke House, Campsbourne Road, London
N8 7PT.

Procter & Procter Ltd, Grayton House, 498 Fulham Road,
London SW6 5NH.

Profiles, 59 Harrow Lane, Maidenhead, Berkshire SL6 7NY.

Salestalk Ltd, Princes Street, Bexleyheath, Kent DA7 4BJ.

Teleforce, 9–11 New Broadway, Ealing, London W5 2NH.

Teleproms, 95 High Street, Burnham, Buckinghamshire SL1
7JZ.

Index